AF876730

Chinese Rule of Law Path and Cultivation of Foreign-Related Rule of Law Talents

Xiaobo Dong · Jie Guo

Chinese Rule of Law Path and Cultivation of Foreign-Related Rule of Law Talents

Springer

Xiaobo Dong
Nanjing Normal University
Nanjing, Jiangsu, China

Jilin International Studies University
Changchun, Jilin, China

Jie Guo
Nanjing Normal University
Nanjing, Jiangsu, China

ISBN 978-981-97-2312-6 ISBN 978-981-97-2313-3 (eBook)
https://doi.org/10.1007/978-981-97-2313-3

The work is sponsored by the Major Cultivation Program of Nanjing Normal University in 2023, entitled "Research on the Translation and Spreading of Excellent Traditional Chinese Legal Culture" (Program No. 23ZD07).

© The Editor(s) (if applicable) and The Author(s), under exclusive license to Springer Nature Singapore Pte Ltd. 2024

This work is subject to copyright. All rights are solely and exclusively licensed by the Publisher, whether the whole or part of the material is concerned, specifically the rights of translation, reprinting, reuse of illustrations, recitation, broadcasting, reproduction on microfilms or in any other physical way, and transmission or information storage and retrieval, electronic adaptation, computer software, or by similar or dissimilar methodology now known or hereafter developed.
The use of general descriptive names, registered names, trademarks, service marks, etc. in this publication does not imply, even in the absence of a specific statement, that such names are exempt from the relevant protective laws and regulations and therefore free for general use.
The publisher, the authors and the editors are safe to assume that the advice and information in this book are believed to be true and accurate at the date of publication. Neither the publisher nor the authors or the editors give a warranty, expressed or implied, with respect to the material contained herein or for any errors or omissions that may have been made. The publisher remains neutral with regard to jurisdictional claims in published maps and institutional affiliations.

This Springer imprint is published by the registered company Springer Nature Singapore Pte Ltd.
The registered company address is: 152 Beach Road, #21-01/04 Gateway East, Singapore 189721, Singapore

Paper in this product is recyclable.

Preface

Since the founding of the Communist Party of China (CPC) in 1921, the Party has led the Chinese people to carry out the great social revolution, full of great hardship and grandeur. Proceeding from China's national conditions, the Party has successfully opened up and expanded Chinese rule of law path, which is a new path to modernization of the rule of law that corresponds to China's specific national conditions, embodies the nature of socialism, and reflects the objective law of the process of modernization of the rule of law in a civilized society.

As a scientific summary of the practice of socialist rule of law with Chinese characteristics, Chinese Thought on the Rule of Law is a major theoretical achievement that conforms to the requirements of the era of the great rejuvenation of the Chinese nation and provides a knowledge system and practice paradigm for the comprehensive construction of a modern socialist country on the track of the rule of law. The people are the main body and source of strength in the construction of the rule of law. To follow the path of socialist rule of law with Chinese characteristics, we must adhere to the principle of committing to a people-centered approach. People-oriented nature is one of the most important characteristics of Chinese Thought on the Rule of Law. Chinese Thought on the Rule of Law has actively safeguarded the common interests of the international community, promoted the cause of human progress, and contributed Chinese rule of law wisdom to the promotion of global governance reform and the construction of a global community of shared future. As a developing country with rising international status, China could not play its role as a responsible country in the process of global governance and the construction of a global community of shared future without high-quality foreign-related rule of law talents with both political integrity and ability. This book systematically explores the connotation, characteristics, historical process and cultural resources of Chinese rule of law path based on the combination of history and reality, theory and practice. It also comprehensively reveals the overall objectives and promotion models of Chinese rule of law path, theoretically expounds the people-oriented nature of Chinese Thought on the Rule of Law and the global initiatives of Chinese rule of law path, and then focuses on the important guarantee of realizing the global initiatives of Chinese rule of law path—the cultivation of foreign-related rule of law talents.

From this book, readers can grasp the rich connotation of the socialist rule of law with Chinese characteristics.

Nanjing, China Xiaobo Dong

Contents

About the Authors

Xiaobo Dong is a Distinguished Professor of Jilin International Studies University and a Professor at School of Foreign Languages and Cultures of Nanjing Normal University, Deputy Director of the Belt and Road Rule of Law Research Center at Academy of China's Modernization of Rule of Law and Researcher at Jiangsu Academy of Talent Development Strategy. He is also Director and Chief Expert of Jiangsu International Rule of Law Research Center, as well as Chief Expert on major programs of the National Social Science Fund of China. His research interests include history of Sino-west civilization exchanges, legal linguistics, legal translation, language policy and planning, cross-cultural communication, as well as area studies. In recent years, he has published over 250 interdisciplinary academic papers and articles in prominent journals and more than 70 books, including academic monographs, edited volumes, and translations.

Jie Guo is Ph.D. Candidate at School of Foreign Languages and Cultures of Nanjing Normal University and Researcher at Jiangsu International Rule of Law Research Center. Her research interests include legal linguistics, legal translation, and language planning.

Chapter 1
Connotation and Characteristics of Chinese Rule of Law Path

Abstract Chinese rule of law path is the concrete manifestation of Chinese path in the field of the rule of law. It is a correct path to the modernization of the rule of law that is in line with China's national conditions, follows the rule of law, and leads to good governance based on the rule of law. Chinese rule of law path embodies profound historical connotations, reflects the distinct socialist nature, mirrors the objective laws of the process of rule of law modernization, and verifies the inherent character of the development of the rule of law. Since the establishment of the People's Republic of China, especially in the more than 40 years of reform and opening up, the arduous practice of exploring a new path to the modernization of the rule of law with Chinese characteristics has historically formed the overall characteristics of the Chinese rule of law path.

1.1 Introduction

The Communist Party of China (CPC) has succeeded in advancing and expanding Chinese modernization, based on decades of exploration and practice since the founding of the People's Republic of China in 1949, especially since the launch of reform and opening up in 1978. Chinese modernization is socialist modernization pursued under the leadership of the CPC. It contains elements common to the modernization processes of all countries, but it is more characterized by features unique to the Chinese context.

President *Xi Jinping* (2021a; b, c, d) pointed out that as we have upheld and developed socialism with Chinese characteristics and driven coordinated progress in material, political, cultural-ethical, social, and ecological terms, we have pioneered a new and uniquely Chinese modernization path and created a new model for human advancement. Chinese modernization path is a major initiative rich in connotation, profound in thoughts, and strict in logic, involving a wide range of fields such as economy, politics, social culture, ecology, China's relationship with the world, etc., and it is a path proceeding from China's specific situation and realizing modernization in a socialist way (Yang 2015: 257). Therefore, it is not only a modernization path

© The Author(s), under exclusive license to Springer Nature Singapore Pte Ltd. 2024
X. Dong and J. Guo, *Chinese Rule of Law Path and Cultivation of Foreign-Related Rule of Law Talents*, https://doi.org/10.1007/978-981-97-2313-3_1

that adapts to the national conditions and reflects the objective laws of modernization, but also a socialist modernization path with distinctive characteristics of the times and nation. The path of Chinese rule of law modernization, which is the concrete embodiment of Chinese path to modernization in the field of the rule of law, is a right path to modernization of the rule of law which conforms to China's national conditions, follows the law of the rule of law, and leads to good law and governance. It is a major achievement which combines Marxist theory on the rule of law, the reality of China's rule of law construction, and the excellent Chinese traditional legal culture.

1.2 Scientific Connotation of Chinese Rule of Law Path

Chinese rule of law path, with profound scientific foundation, is a socialist path to modernization of the rule of law, the path of Chinese rule of law modernization, and a new path to the civilization of the rule of law of mankind. To be specific, the path of Chinese rule of law modernization has the following connotations.

1. Profound Historical Implications

It was pointed out profoundly by president *Xi Jinping* (2021a; b, c, d) that we must follow our own path—this is the bedrock that underpins all the theories and practices of our Party. More than that, it is the historical conclusion our Party has drawn from its struggles over the past century. In the Resolution of the Central Committee of the Communist Party of China on the Major Achievements and Historical Experience of the Party over the Past Century adopted at the Sixth Plenary Session of the 19th Central Committee of the Communist Party of China on November 11, 2021, "taking the Chinese path" is regarded as one of the valuable historical experiences of the Party's endeavors over the past century. It was pointed out that throughout human history, no nation or country has ever become strong and prosperous by relying on external forces, indiscriminately copying the models of other countries, or blindly following in others' footsteps (Xi 2021a; b, c, d). This important historical experience and scientific judgment is fully applicable to the field of the rule of law and modernization of the rule of law. There is no one-size-fits-all model of rule of law in the world, nor is there a universally applicable road to modernization of the rule of law. Different social and economic conditions, political systems, social structures, cultural traditions, historical foundations, and even geographical environments will inevitably lead to different ways of modernization of the rule of law.

Standing at the height of world history, Chinese Thought on the Rule of Law observes the development process of the rule of law in human society "through the prism of historical laws (Xi 2017b: 128) and explores the path of the rule of law suitable for China. In contemporary China, Chinese Communists explore and develop the appropriate rule of law from the practice of China's revolution, construction and reform, and open up the path of Chinese rule of law modernization in light of the Chinese context and the requirements of the times. President *Xi Jinping* deeply grasped the conditions and characteristics of national conditions in China, deeply investigated the historical movement of the evolution of the national system and legal system under China's national conditions and stressed that China is working to achieve modernization for more than 1.4 billion people, a number larger than the combined population of all developed countries in the world today. This is a task of unparalleled difficulty and complexity; it inevitably means that our pathways of development and methods of advancement will be unique. We will, as always, bear China's realities in mind as we address issues, make decisions, and take action. We will neither pursue grandiose goals nor go by the rule book. We will stay patient in advancing the course of history and take steady and incremental steps to sustain progress (Xi 2022a, b).

China has always been one of the world's great countries, and the laws of ancient China have extensive influence and spread to neighboring countries and other countries in the world. However, after the Opium War in 1840, China was gradually reduced to a semi-colonial, semi-feudal society, and the autonomy process of Chinese legal development was interrupted. In order to change the future and destiny of the Chinese nation, countless dedicated patriots tried every possible means to seek a political and legal development path suitable for the characteristics of their national conditions. Various institutional models such as constitutional monarchy, parliamentary system, multi-party system, and presidential system and so on had been tried in modem China, but all ended in failure (Xi 2020: 262). Facts had proved that all these systems were unfeasible in China and failed to provide institutional guarantee for realizing national prosperity and people's happiness. At last, China opted for the path of Chinese rule of law modernization. The CPC, since its founding a century ago, has followed the rule of law, adhered to the combination of Marxist theory on the rule of law with China's specific national conditions and with China's excellent traditional legal culture, made unremitting efforts to build a socialist national system and legal system with Chinese characteristics, and opened up a path of modernization to the rule of law with distinctive Chinese characteristics.

It should be noted that the unique cultural tradition doomed China to take the path of modernization to the rule of law suitable for its own characteristics. China is a country with ancient and great civilization in the world. In the long process of the development of Chinese civilization for more than 5000 years, the Chinese nation has forged a broad and profound legal culture that embodies the unique national legal character. There are many thoughts and ideas that transcend time and space and have universal value worthy of inheritance and development. In contemporary China, adhering to and expanding the path of Chinese rule of law modernization is, to a large extent, a process of creative transformation and innovative development of Chinese excellent traditional legal culture, the cultural fertile soil on which the path of Chinese rule of law modernization depends to form and develop. The CPC has opened up a new path of Chinese rule of law modernization in the long-term practical exploration, which is by no means accidental, but determined by China's historical inheritance and cultural tradition.

2. Distinctive Socialist Nature

Chinese rule of law path is not a copy of the western capitalist path to the rule of law, but a socialist path of the rule of law with Chinese characteristics. The socialist path of the rule of law with Chinese characteristics that we will adhere to is essentially the concrete embodiment of the socialist path with Chinese characteristics in the field of rule of law; the socialist theory of the rule of law with Chinese characteristics that we will develop is essentially the theoretical achievement of the theoretical system of socialism with Chinese characteristics on the issue of the rule of law; the socialist system of the rule of law with Chinese characteristics that we will build is essentially the legal manifestation of the socialist system with Chinese characteristics (Xi 2021c). Specifically speaking about the achievements in our country's rule of law construction, there are dozens of examples that can be listed, big and small. However, they can be summarized by saying that we have embarked on the path of socialist rule of law with Chinese characteristics (Xi 2020: 165). The socialist path of the rule of law with Chinese characteristics is the only correct path to modernization of the rule of law in China, highlighting the socialist nature of modernization of the rule of law with Chinese characteristics.

The leadership of the CPC is the fundamental guarantee for modernization of the rule of law in China. Since its founding a century ago, the CPC has taken a remarkable journey. The CPC has dedicated to uniting and leading the people through arduous and magnificent struggles, opening up and expanding the path of Chinese rule of law modernization, and writing a magnificent chapter for socialism with Chinese characteristics in the new era. Scientific socialism has radiated strong vitality in China, bringing about major changes in the historical evolution and competition of the two ideologies and social systems of socialism and capitalism in the world in favor of socialism (2021a; b, c, d). From the perspective of the organic unity of history and reality, domestic and international conditions, theory and practice, Chinese Communists profoundly summarized the historical lessons of the world socialist movement and the socialist rule of law since the founding of New China, made a series of strategic arrangements for the development of in socialist rule of law with Chinese characteristics, fully demonstrating the socialist nature of Chinese path to modernization of the rule of law with Chinese characteristics. Chinese socialist modernization of the rule of law in the twenty-first century has given rise to strong vitality, made significant historical contributions to the socialist modernization of the rule of law in the twenty-first century, and contributed Chinese wisdom to the exploration and construction of a better social system for mankind.

The socialist system with Chinese characteristics is the fundamental cornerstone of the path of Chinese rule of law modernization. In contemporary China, emphasis should be laid upon grasping the nature and characteristics of the national political system to correctly understand the socialist nature of the path of Chinese rule of law modernization. Since the launch of reform and opening up, the Party has led the people in keeping to the path of socialist political advancement with Chinese characteristics and developing socialist democracy and has achieved substantial progress in this regard. Learning lessons from successes and failures in political development both at home and abroad, the Party has become deeply aware of the following: to have full confidence in the system of socialism with Chinese characteristics, we must first and foremost foster strong confidence in the political system of socialism with Chinese characteristics; to promote socialist democracy and socialist political advancement, we must ensure that the political system of socialism with Chinese characteristics is deeply rooted in China (2021a; b, c, d).

The political system of a country is the primary and decisive factors in the modernization of the rule of law in this country. The CPC is the leading core of the cause of socialism with Chinese characteristics. Adhering to and improving the Party's leadership system and strengthening the Party's leadership over the construction of the national system and legal system are the fundamental systems in the socialist system with Chinese characteristics, which fundamentally determine the basic nature of the path of Chinese rule of law modernization.

The socialist political system with Chinese characteristics endows Chinese rule of law path with a distinctive socialist nature. From the perspective of the basic economic system, the co-development of multiple forms of ownership with public ownership playing a dominant role, the co-existence of multiple modes of distribution with distribution according to the amount of labor performed playing a dominant role, the system of socialist market economy, and other basic socialist economic regimes highlight the advantages of the socialist system, thus forming the economic foundation of the path of Chinese rule of law modernization. In addition, in the process of adhering to and developing socialism with Chinese characteristics, promoting common prosperity and promoting social fairness and justice reflect the essential nature and fundamental purpose of socialism and the distinct direction of the path of Chinese rule of law modernization. Common prosperity is the essential requirement of socialism and an important feature of Chinese modernization path (Xi 2021c). The socialist nature of modernization of the rule of law in China inevitably requires that the development of the rule of law in contemporary China always focuses on and earnestly addresses the promotion of common prosperity and the maintenance of social fairness and justice. It is essential to prioritize the construction of the rule of law system that plays a significant role in promoting common prosperity and advancing social fairness and justice, so as to lay a solid foundation of the rule of law values for upholding and expanding the path of Chinese rule of law modernization.

Committing to a people-centered approach is the fundamental value of Chinese modernization of the rule of law. China's state system is a socialist country led by the working class and based on the alliance of workers and peasants, which is in essence the dictatorship of the proletariat. This state system determines that all the power of the country belongs to the people. The implementation of the system of people's congresses in China is the great creation of the Chinese people in the history of human political system (Xi 2014b: 4). State administrative organs, supervisory organs, judicial organs and procuratorial organs are all created by the People's Congress in accordance with the procedures prescribed by the Constitution and laws. The executive power, supervisory power and judicial power are derived from the organs of state power, so as to ensure that all state powers are ultimately exercised by the people. Therefore, President *Xi Jinping* (Xi 2022a, b) stressed that the socialist rule of law system with Chinese characteristics is an important part of the socialist system with Chinese characteristics. We must firmly grasp the nature of socialism with Chinese characteristics and unswervingly follow the path of socialist rule of law with Chinese characteristics. We must be particularly clear and firm on major issues such as adhering to the comprehensive leadership of the Party and ensuring that the country is governed by the people.

3. Reflection of the Objective Laws of Modernization of the Rule of Law

According to the basic principles of Marxist historical materialism, the historical development of human society is by no means a pile of accidental events, but a regular process of movement. Similarly, modernization is the historical replacement of the traditional way of life and its system to the modern way of life and its system. This historic leap has led to great innovation in the value system of the whole civilization. This process is not only a worldwide phenomenon, but also a worldwide historical process and a phenomenon with strong national style. Therefore, modernization is the organic unity of universality and particularity. Modernization of the rule of law, with its inherent laws of movement, is a profound revolution in the process of the development of law in a civilized society.

The path of Chinese rule of law modernization is the product of certain social and historical conditions, which profoundly reflects the basic trend and internal rules of modernization of the rule of law in a civilized society. From the perspective of the historical trend of Chinese modernization of the rule of law, the development process of human civilization has objectively formed different historical forms of the development of law. Different types of legal development have different value objectives. The modernization of the rule of law is the process of the growth and leap forward in human legal civilization and a profound revolution in the process of the development of law in a civilized society, reflecting the exciting picture of the legal reform in the specific stage of the transformation from a pre-modern society to a modern society. In China, a developing socialist eastern country with a vast territory, a large population, numerous nationalities and complex national conditions, modernization of the rule of law is a process of the rule of law reform displayed under the specific national conditions of China. Chinese modernization of the rule of law is a historic change in the evolution of China's legal civilization, which embodies its unique internal logic. In contemporary China, Chinese Communists, from the strategic height of ensuring the long-term stability of the party and the country, have a deep understanding of important roles of the rule of law in the process of national modernization, combine the basic principles of the Marxist theory on the rule of law with China's specific conditions, and with Chinese excellent traditional legal culture, and independently and successfully create, adhere to, and expand a new path of Chinese rule of law modernization suitable for China's national conditions.

To evaluate the modernization of the rule of law in a society, it is important to examine the level of the rule of law in that country. A country that has achieved modernization of the rule of law must be a country ruled by law. In contemporary China, the modernization of the rule of law is a multifaceted process including legal thoughts, legal systems, legal acts, legal practices, and so on, which constitutes an important part of the modernization of the national governance system and governance capacity. Since the 18th CPC National Congress, the CPC Central Committee with Comrade *Xi Jinping* as the core has grasped the strategic position of adhering to the overall law-based governance from the strategic overall situation of the country's modernization construction in the new era, summarized the strategic overall situation of the path of Chinese rule of law modernization, put forward the major strategic tasks of adhering to and improving the socialist system with Chinese characteristics, and promote the modernization of the country's governance system and capacity, which deeply reflects the inevitable requirement of adhering to and developing socialism with Chinese characteristics, and aims to promote the socialist system with Chinese characteristics to be more mature, so as to provide a more complete, more stable and effective system for the long-term stability of the Party and the country. This is an extremely grand social project that requires comprehensive and deepening reforms to promote the modernization of the national governance system and governance capacity in all fields. President *Xi Jinping* pointed out that law is the most important tool for governing the country, and the rule of law is an important support for the country's governance system and capacity (Xi 2020: 85). Therefore, as an important part of the modernization of national governance, promoting modernization of the rule of law is to realize the historical transformation from the traditional national governance system of rule of man to the modern national governance system of rule of law. To adhere to the new path to modernization of the rule of law with Chinese characteristics, we must accelerate the construction of the socialist rule of law system with Chinese characteristics and strive to improve the effectiveness of the rule of law in promoting the modernization of the country's governance system and governance capacity. Realizing the modernization of the rule of law in China and building a national governance system based on the rule of law is the internal need to further promote the modernization of national governance.

Having a glimpse of the historical process of modernization of rule of law in the world, we can see that the modernization of the rule of law is a universal historical process in the world and constitutes the main theme of the reform and development of the country and the field of the rule of law since modern times. However, this process has different historical characteristics in different countries, and thus forms different patterns of modernization of the rule of law. Therefore, the modernization of the rule of law is a process of diversity and unity of legal development. The legal development of different nations or countries always follows a specific path under the influence of different conditions. Within the same social formation, the economic, cultural and ideological development levels of different countries inconsistent. They also have differences in their national forms and political systems. Each country has its own specific historical development, customs and national traditional characteristics. Furthermore, these countries are located in different geographical positions, with varying natural conditions and population situations. These complex factors are bound to make the process of modernization of the rule of law in a civilized society show rich and diverse historical characteristics. Under the influence of the level of economic development, cultural tradition, geographical environment and other factors, the development of the rule of law in different regions of contemporary China has formed certain differences. Therefore, the development of the rule of law in China has a pattern of unity and diversity, which reflects the richness and diversity of the modernization process of the rule of law in China, and also deeply reflects the law of unbalanced development of China, an eastern power. We must follow this rule, and on the premise of adhering to the unity of the national rule of law, starting from the reality of economic development in different regions, make full use of the rule of law to promote regional economic and social development, promote modernization of regional social governance, and promote the organic combination of regional rule of law development based on administrative divisions and regional rule of law development based on cross-administrative regions to establish the strategic direction for opening a new era and comprehensively promoting the new journey of Chinese modernization of the rule of law.

4. Confirmation of Inherent Character of Chinese Rule of Law Path

Generally speaking, the development of the rule of law can be differentiated into independent and dependent development of the rule of law based on whether the development of the rule of law conforms to the national conditions. These two different types of development of the rule of law reflect that the different positions of countries or regions in the process of development of the rule of law, which may even be asymmetric or unequal. The development of independent rule of law refers to the independent choice of the rule of law development mode suitable for the country's social and living conditions based on the profound understanding of the country's national conditions, and subsequently steadily advancing process of the rule of law modernization. On the other hand, the development of dependent rule of law refers to the development and implementation of the rule of law construction programs by some developing countries in accordance with the legal system model of foreign countries (mainly western countries), in order to make the development of their own rule of law dependent on the legal system of foreign countries. Obviously, these two different development models of the rule of law will inevitably lead to two distinctly different outcomes of the development of the rule of law.

In the new era of reconstructing the global order, legal life in China is increasingly intertwined and interacted with that in the world. How can the reform and development of the rule of law in contemporary China maintain its independent and autonomous character and avoid the marginalization of the dependent reform and development of the rule of law? This is a significant challenge we must confront in this era. Since entering the new historical period of reform and opening up, *Deng Xiaoping* (1994: 163) has repeatedly stressed that in our democratic revolution, we had to act in accordance with China's specific situation and follow the path discovered by Comrade *Mao Zedong* of encircling the cities from the rural areas. Now, in our national construction, we must likewise act in accordance with out own situation and find a Chinese modernization path. He also pointed out that none of the works of *Karl Marx* or of *Lenin* offers a guide for building socialism in China, and conditions differ from one country to another, each having its own unique experience. So, we have to think for ourselves. This is true not only in economic matters but also in political matters (Deng 1994a, b: 261).

The development of the rule of law in China is the reform and innovative practice of the rule of law system, rule of law system and rule of law mechanism under specific time and space conditions, with unique historical traditions and social conditions. Since the 18th National Congress of the Communist Party of China, facing the development trend of the contemporary globalization movement and various new situations and new problems, *Xi Jinping* (2014c: 29), from the strategic orientation of adhering to and developing socialism with Chinese characteristics, further pointed out that independence is the inevitable conclusion of our Party's revolution, construction and reform based on China's reality and relying on the strength of the Party and the people. Regardless of the past, present and future, we should put the development of the country and the nation on the basis of our own strength, adhere to national pride and self-confidence, and unswervingly follow our own path. Independence is an inevitable conclusion drawn by our Party from China's reality, after going through the stages of revolution, development and reform by relying on the strength of the Party and the people. We should always rely on ourselves when seeking our national development and defending our national pride and confidence, and resolutely follow our own road now and in the future as we did in the past. Adhering to independence means that Chinese affairs must be dealt with and decided by the Chinese people themselves. There is no such thing in the world as a development model that can be applied universally, nor is there any development path that remains carved in stone. The diversity of historical conditions determines the diversity of the development paths chosen by various countries. In the whole history of mankind, no nation or state has ever been able to rise to power and rejuvenate itself by relying solely on external forces or blindly following others; doing so inevitably leads to failure or subservience.

More than 70 years after the founding of New China, especially more than 40 years after the reform and opening up, Chinese Communists have combined the Marxist theory on the rule of law with China's specific reality, independently choosing their own path to the development of the rule of law, and constantly deepening their understanding of the rule of law of the CPC, the law of socialist rule of law construction, and the law of human society development. Efforts have been made to create a socialist state system and legal system with distinctive Chinese characteristics, thus giving full play to the vigorous vitality of the cause of the socialist rule of law with Chinese characteristics, opening up a Chinese rule of law path, and building a solid institutional foundation for the "rule of China". Chinese model of modernization of the rule of law, which is gradually formed in the process of contemporary Chinese society and rule of law reform, has its own unique historical personality and distinct Chinese characteristics. As emphasized in the Resolution of the Sixth Plenary Session of the 19th Central Committee of the Communist Party of China, independence is the essence of China's national spirit, and it is a major principle for building our Party and our country. We must follow our own path—this is the historical conclusion our Party has drawn from its endeavors over the past century (2021a; b, c, d).

1.3 Overall Characteristics of Chinese Rule of Law Path

In leading the Chinese people in the great and arduous social struggle, Chinese Communists adhere to the combination of Marxist theory on the rule of law with China's specific reality and with Chinese excellent traditional legal culture, striving to find a new path of modernization to the rule of law with distinctive Chinese characteristics. As *Xi Jinping* (2020: 110) pointed out, what kind of rule of law path to take and what kind of rule of law system to build are determined by the basic national conditions of a country. The conditions or factors in China's social economy, politics, culture, history and geographical environment determine or restrict the basic orientation and movement direction of Chinese modernization of the rule of law. Over the past 70 years since the founding of the People's Republic of China, the arduous practice of exploring the new path of rule of law modernization with Chinese characteristics has historically generated the comprehensive characteristics of China's solution to rule of law modernization.

1. Political Guarantee—Leadership of the Party

In contemporary China, as the highest political leadership of the country, the CPC, in a leading position in the whole country and social life, shall uphold and strengthen the Party's leadership in advancing law-based governance in all fields, which is the fundamental political guarantee for Chinese modernization of the rule of law. The purpose of comprehensively deepening reform, building law-based China and strengthening the construction of the national system and national governance system is to continuously promote the self-improvement and development of the socialist system with Chinese characteristics. Among them, the core is to uphold and improve the Party's leadership. Therefore, the leadership of the Party is the most fundamental guarantee for advancing law-based governance in all fields and realizing Chinese modernization of the rule of law.

We shall adhere to and strengthen the Party's leadership for advancing overall law-based governance and ensure the correct direction for building law-based China and promoting the modernization of Chinese rule of law. Adhering to the Party's leadership in the advancing overall law-based governance should be embodied in the Party's leadership in legislation, ensuring law enforcement, supporting the judiciary, and taking the lead in abiding by the law. For one thing, we shall give full play to the leading role of the Party in taking the overall picture and coordinating all parties, comprehensively coordinate the work of governing the country according to law in all fields, and implement the Party's leadership in the whole process and all aspects of law-based governance. For another, we shall improve the Party's leadership in advancing overall law-based governance and improve its working mechanisms for exercising law-based governance (Xi 2019). We shall consciously act within the scope of the Constitution and laws, and constantly improve the Party's ability and level of governing the country and ruling by law.

2. Theoretical Guidance—Chinese Thought on the Rule of Law

Chinese Thought on the Rule of Law is broad and profound, rich in content, strict in logic, and complete in system. From the combination of theory and practice, it has scientifically answered a series of important questions on adhering to and expanding Chinese rule of law path and has established a logic system of Marxist theory on the rule of law with original significance in the twenty-first century, which is the theoretical guidance to the promotion of Chinese modernization of the rule of law.

Chinese Thought on the Rule of Law creatively discusses the strategic position of promoting Chinese modernization of the rule of law. Since the founding of the Party, the CPC has led the Chinese people to carry out a great social revolution that is arduous and magnificent. Proceeding from China's national conditions, it has successfully opened up and expanded Chinese rule of law path.

Chinese Thought on the Rule of Law creatively reveals the national conditions for promoting the modernization of Chinese rule of law. The biggest national condition of China is the leadership of the CPC. The leadership of the CPC is the most essential feature of socialism with Chinese characteristics. As General Secretary *Xi Jinping* (2017a: 28) said, what is Chinese characteristics? This is Chinese characteristics. The system led by the CPC is our own, not cloned from anywhere, nor imitated by others. Adhering to and improving the Party's leadership system and strengthening the Party's leadership over the construction of the national system and legal system are the fundamental political guarantee for promoting the modernization of Chinese rule of law.

Chinese Thought on the Rule of Law creatively analyzes the internal motivation of promoting Chinese rule of law modernization. First, actively responding to the new needs of the people for the rule of law. The starting point and destination of promoting Chinese rule of law modernization in the new era is to keep abreast of the new changes in the main contradictions in China's society, carefully grasp the new needs and expectations of the people for the construction of the rule of law, and adhere to whether the people are satisfied and have a "sense of gain" to test the success and failure of the overall law-based governance. Second, continuously developing whole-process people's democracy. General Secretary *Xi Jinping* creatively expounded the Marxist theory on state and law, scientifically revealed the development law of socialist democracy with Chinese characteristics and put forward the major idea of "developing whole-process people's democracy". Third, unswervingly promoting reform in the field of the rule of law. Since the 18th National Congress of the Communist Party of China, under the guidance of Chinese Thought on the Rule of Law, historical changes have taken place and historic achievements have been made in the field of rule of law in the new era, effectively promoting the continuous development of modernization of Chinese rule of law.

3. Value Orientation—Committing to a People-centered Approach

To advance law-based governance and build law-based China, we shall adhere to the people-centered rule of law development guidelines, and earnestly safeguard and promote social fairness and justice. This is the basic value orientation of the modernization of Chinese rule of law. The people-oriented nature of the rule of law is the fundamental difference between Chinese modernization of the rule of law and capitalist modernization of the rule of law. In the historical process of advancing the Chinese modernization of the rule of law, we shall adhere to the people's principal position, adhere to the most distinctive character of Marxism—the people-oriented nature, and continue to promote the construction of people's democracy throughout the process (Xi 2021a: 336). We will continue to strengthen the institutional guarantee that the people are the masters of the country, and uphold the rule of law for the people, rely on the people, benefit the people, and protect the people. We must firmly grasp the value pursuit of social fairness and justice and strive to make the people feel fairness and justice in every legal system, every law enforcement decision, and every judicial case (Xi 2019). Social fairness and justice cover the value ideal of socialism, embody the essential attribute of the socialist system, and constitute the ultimate support of the social value system. The legal system is the carrier of fairness and justice. Justice is the lifeline of the rule of law (Xi 2017a: 101).

To comprehensively administer the country in accordance with law, we must closely focus on safeguarding and promoting social fairness and justice, give full play to the interest adjustment function of the rule of law, reasonably balance and adjust the different interests of different social groups, and effectively safeguard and realize the development rights and interests of the overwhelming majority of the people. To comprehensively deepen reform, we must focus on creating a more fair and just social environment, constantly overcome all kinds of phenomena that violate fairness and justice, and make the results of reform and development more and more equitable for all people (Xi 2014a: 96). Therefore, we shall take the maintenance and realization of social fairness and justice as the basic value criterion for the construction of the rule of law, strive to grasp the people's recognition of the construction of the rule of law, adhere to whether the people are satisfied and have a "sense of gain" to test the success or failure of the development of the rule of law, and fully mobilize the enthusiasm and initiative of the people to participate in the construction of the rule of law.

4. Strategic Goal—Building Rule of Law China with Good Law and Good Governance

There are various models of rule of law in the world. The people of the CPC systematically investigated and deeply reflected on various models of rule of law at all times and in all over the world. On this basis, they firmly established the concept of "good law and good governance", emphasized the socialist road of rule of law with Chinese characteristics, and built a rule of law China with good law and good governance. In 2014, it was put forward in the Decision of the Central Committee of the Communist Party of China on several major issues concerning comprehensively promoting the rule of law that law is the most important tool for governing the country, and good law is the prerequisite for good governance. In the Decision, President *Xi Jinping* (2020: 20) pointed that with ongoing progress being made in the socialist legal system with Chinese characteristics and a stronger sense of rule of law across society, the people have raised their expectations for legislation from whether there is a law to follow to whether they will benefit from the law and whether it is effective enough to solve problems. They have expressed earnest expectations for us to oversee and rectify normative documents in violation of the Constitution and the law and protect their legitimate rights and interests through recording, review and oversight.

In the report delivered at the 19th National Congress of the Communist Party of China, General Secretary *Xi Jinping* (2017a; b, c) stressed that we will strengthen oversight to ensure compliance with the Constitution, advance constitutionality review, and safeguard the authority of the Constitution. We will carry out lawmaking in a well-conceived and democratic way and in accordance with law, so that good laws are made to promote development and ensure good governance. In 2018, President *Xi Jinping* (2020: 236) emphasized at the first meeting of the Central Committee for Comprehensive Rule of Law that we shall promote the penetration of socialist core values in all aspects of legislation, law enforcement, justice and law-abiding, so that the socialist rule of law can become good law and good governance.

In order to build law-based China with good law and good governance, we insist on integrating socialist core values into legislation, striving to make every legislation conform to the spirit of the Constitution, reflect the will of the people, and win the support of the people; We shall also integrate the core socialist values into law enforcement and justice, adhere to strict law enforcement, promote the true, the good and the beautiful, and punish the false, the evil and the ugly, adhere to fair justice, give full play to the functions of judicial division to stop disputes, and punish the evil and promote the good. In accordance with the basic requirements of socialist core values, we are improving regulations and systems across all fields, enhancing citizen conventions, community regulations, student codes of conduct, and other behavioral guidelines. We aim to make socialist core values the fundamental guiding principles for people's daily work and life, striving to cultivate a positive social atmosphere and maintain social order.

5. Path Choice—Advancing Overall Law-based Governance

Advancing overall law-based governance is the practical choice to promote Chinese rule of law modernization and the only way to realize the modernization of Chinese rule of law. Advancing overall law-based governance is a systematic project. We shall make overall consideration, grasp the key points, make overall planning, and pay more attention to the system, integrity, and synergy (Xi 2020: 229).

President *Xi Jinping* (2020: 112) applied the systematic concept of Marxist philosophy as the basic thought and working method to the field of rule of law, and proposed that adhering to the principle of pursuing coordinated progress in law-based governance, law-based exercise of state power, and law-based government administration, and promoting the integrated development of rule of law for the country, the government, and society, which fully expresses the overall view of the development of the rule of law in contemporary China. Thus, it is important to correctly understand and deal with the major dialectical relations in the process of advancing overall law-based governance. President *Xi Jinping* (2019) regards handling the dialectical relationship of advancing overall law-based governance as an organic component of advancing overall law-based governance, pointing out that to advance law-based governance in all fields, we shall correctly handle the relationship between politics and the rule of law, reform and the rule of law, rule of law and rule of virtue, rule of law and rule of the party.

Therefore, to adhere to and apply the dialectics of overall law-based governance, we shall pay attention to observing and understanding the development trend of China and the world in the process of Chinese rule of law modernization from the perspective of universal connection, focus on the domestic and international overall situation, and deeply consider and study the strategic overall situation and target selection of the path of Chinese rule of law modernization; we shall pay attention to and use the perspective of development to deeply analyze the historical basis, objective reality and future trend of promoting Chinese rule of law modernization, and grasp a number of fundamental, overall and strategic issues related to the rule of law, so as to lead the era process of China's construction of rule of law; we shall pay attention to the use of the basic laws and methods of the unity of opposites to deeply and systematically analyze various contradictory relations in the process of Chinese modernization of the rule of law, especially to have a deep understanding of the dialectical unity relations between politics and the rule of law, reform and the rule of law, rule of law and rule of virtue, rule of law and rule of the party, so as to adhere to the correct direction and display the "Chinese logic" of modernization of the rule of law.

6. Global Orientation—Building a Global Community of Shared Future

The era process of the contemporary CPC to expand the new path of Chinese rule of law modernization is intrinsically intertwined with the great changes in the world's rule of law civilization, which historically reshapes the development pattern of the world's rule of law civilization and contains the basic value elements of the new form of human rule of law civilization. This is the global orientation of Chinese rule of law path. Civilized diversity is the basic feature of human society and the inexhaustible driving force of human progress. The diversity of civilizations determines the inherent inevitability of exchanges and mutual learning among civilizations.

President *Xi Jinping* (2018: 76) stressed that human civilizations have the value of exchange and mutual learning because of their diversity. The exchange and mutual learning of civilizations are important driving forces to promote the progress of human civilization and the peaceful development of the world. Different countries and nations, regardless of social systems, values and development paths, or historical traditions, religious beliefs and cultural backgrounds, have differences, which is the inevitable result of historical development. The development of one civilization does not exclude the development of other civilizations, nor does it necessarily presuppose the decline of other civilizations. All countries and nationalities have made contributions to the development of human civilization. The development of various civilizations can go hand in hand and interact, influence, absorb and integrate with each other. Each civilization will draw nutrients from other civilizations, and at the same time, it will exert different degrees of influence on other civilizations. Standing at the new historical starting point of promoting the construction of a global community of shared future, *Xi Jinping* (2021a; b, c, d) clearly expounded the common values of all mankind and stressed the need to carry forward the common values of all mankind, including peace, development, fairness, justice, democracy and freedom. The initiative of the common values of all mankind conforms to the historical trend of the progress of human civilization and leads the evolution direction of the development of legal civilization in the world.

Faced with the question of the century "what has happened to the world and how should we respond?", *Xi Jinping* creatively put forward the major strategic idea of promoting the construction of a global community of shared future, proposing five aspects of emphasis: (1) We shall adhere to equality-based dialogue and friendly consultations, build a world of lasting peace, promote fair and just global governance, and jointly promote the democratization of international relations; (2) We shall adhere to the principle of collaboration and sharing, build a world that enjoys universal security, jointly promote the rule of law in international relations, safeguard the authority of the international rule of law, oppose the act of dividing the legitimate rights and interests of other countries in the name of "rule of law", and undermine national peace and stability. No country can launch war at will, nor undermine the international rule of law, and strive to achieve common, comprehensive, cooperative and sustainable security; (3) We shall adhere to win–win cooperation, build a world of common prosperity, work together to rationalize international relations, improve the position and role of developing countries in the global governance system, and promote the construction of an open, inclusive, balanced, and win–win economic globalization. The proposal and implementation of the Belt and Road Initiative is to implement the concept of a global community of shared future; (4) We shall adhere to exchanges and mutual benefits and build an open and inclusive world. All human civilizations are equal in value. Civilizations vary from each other only as human beings differ in terms of skin color and the language used. No civilization is superior to others; (5) We shall build a clean and beautiful world, protect the only earth home on which mankind depends for survival, and jointly build a community of human and natural life. The proposal and practice of the major strategic idea of promoting the building of a global community of shared future has profoundly reflected the historic changes in the relationship between China and the world in the new era and has formed a strong international influence.

1.4 Conclusion

Chinese rule of law path is a path of modernization of the rule of law that corresponds to specific national conditions in China, reflects the nature of socialism, and reflects the objective law of the process of modernization of the rule of law in a civilized society. We shall correctly grasp the connotation and characteristics of Chinese path to modernization of the rule of law, and promote the connection between the path of Chinese rule of law modernization and the path of world rule of law civilization. The significance of the new path of Chinese rule of law modernization is not only that it is the correct path and the only way for Chinese rule of law modernization, but also that it has opened up a new path for developing countries to move towards the modernization of the rule of law, providing more and more fresh experience for developing countries to solve the problems of rule of law and smoothly move towards the modernization of the rule of law.

References

Deng, X. 1994a. *Selected works of Deng Xiaoping II*. People's Publishing House.

Deng, X. 1994b. *Selected works of Deng Xiaoping III*. People's Publishing House.

The Communist Party of China (CPC) Central Committee. 2021. *Resolution of the Central Committee of the Communist Party of China on the major achievements and historical experience of the Party over the past century*. People's Publishing House.

Xi, J. 2014a. *Excerpts from Xi Jinping's discussion on comprehensively deepening reform*. Central Party Literature Press.

Xi, J. 2014b. *Speech at the 60th anniversary of the national people's congress of the People's Republic of China*. People's Publishing House.

Xi, J. 2014c. *Xi Jinping: The governance of China I*. Foreign Language Press.

Xi, J. 2017a. *Excerpts from Xi Jinping's discussion on socialist political construction*. Central Party Literature Press.

Xi, J. 2017b. Secure a decisive victory in building a moderately prosperous society in all respects and strive for the great success of socialism with Chinese characteristics for a new era. *People's Daily*, October 28.

Xi, J. 2017c. *Xi Jinping: The governance of China II*. Foreign Language Press. Central Party Literature Press.

Xi, J. 2018. *On building a global community of shared future*. Central Party Literature Press.

Xi, J. 2019. Strengthen the leadership of the Communist Party of China (CPC) in advancing overall law-based governance. *Qiushi*, 4.

Xi, J. 2020. *On adhering to overall law-based governance of China*. Central Party Literature Press.

Xi, J. 2021a. Firmly taking the socialist rule of law path with Chinese characteristics in the new era to provide support for building a modern socialist country in all respects. *Qiushi*, 5, 4–6.

Xi, J. 2021b. Make solid progress in promoting common prosperity. *Qiushi*, 20.

Xi, J. 2021c. *People are the masters of the country*. Central Party Literature Press.

Xi, J. 2021d. Speech at a ceremony marking the centenary of the Communist Party of China. *People's Daily*, July 2.

Xi, J. 2022a. Adhere to the path of socialist rule of law with Chinese characteristics and better promote the construction of socialist rule of law system with Chinese Characteristics. *Qiushi*, 4.

Xi, J. 2022b. Hold high the great banner of socialism with Chinese characteristics and strive in unity to build a modern socialist country in all respects—Report to the 20th national congress of the Communist Party of China. *People's Daily*, October 26.

Yang, G. 2015. *The rise of the East: Philosophical reflections on Chinese path to modernization*. Beijing Normal University Press.

Chapter 2
Historical Process of Chinese Rule of Law Path

Abstract The historical process of Chinese rule of law path reflects, in a concentrated manner, the profound revolutions in the country and social life. It embodies the direction of the national modernization process, and historically verifies the great leap of the Chinese nation, which since modern times began had endured so much for so long, has achieved a tremendous transformation: It has stood up, become better off, and grown in strength.

2.1 Introduction

In the speech at the ceremony marking the centenary of the Communist Party of China, General Secretary *Xi Jinping* (Xi 2021a, b) comprehensively reviewed the glorious course of the CPC's centennial struggle, which was accurately divided into four historical periods, that is, to realize national rejuvenation, the Party united and led the Chinese people in fighting bloody battles with unyielding determination, achieving great success in the new-democratic revolution, in socialist revolution and construction, in reform, opening up, and socialist modernization and in socialism with Chinese characteristics in the new era.

Resolution of the Central Committee of the Communist Party of China on the major achievements and historical experience of the Party over the past century, which was adopted at the Sixth Plenary Session of the 19th Central Committee of the Communist Party of China on November 11, 2021, reviewed and summarized the great and momentous centennial course of the Party's struggle, and divided the centennial course of revolution, construction and reform led by the Party into and four historical periods that are both related and different: the new democratic revolution, the socialist revolution and the promotion of socialist construction, the reform and opening up, socialist modernization, and socialism with Chinese characteristics in the new era (Xi 2021a, b). Since the very day of its founding, the Party has led the people to firmly promote the magnificent social revolution, creating miracle upon miracle that has stood out in the annals of history (Xi 2017: 12) and creating a new path of Chinese rule of law modernization. In connection with the four historical

© The Author(s), under exclusive license to Springer Nature Singapore Pte Ltd. 2024

X. Dong and J. Guo, *Chinese Rule of Law Path and Cultivation of Foreign-Related Rule of Law Talents*, https://doi.org/10.1007/978-981-97-2313-3_2

periods mentioned above, the development process of the new path of Chinese rule of law modernization can be divided into the following four stages: the construction of the new democratic revolutionary legal system, reflecting the early exploration of the new path to the modernization of Chinese rule of law; the development of the rule of law in the period of socialist revolution and construction, laying a preliminary foundation for the formation of a new path to modernization of Chinese rule of law; the new great social revolution of reform and opening up, strongly promoting the formation of a new path to modernization of Chinese rule of law; the construction of China under the rule of law in the new era of socialism with Chinese characteristics, marking the further expansion of the new path of Chinese rule of law modernization. This chapter intends to make a general preliminary investigation of the formation and development process of Chinese rule of law path, so as to reveal the movement track of the new path of Chinese rule of law modernization.

2.2 Early Exploration of Chinese Rule of Law Path

Reviewing the legal development process in modern China, whether it is the legal reform in the late Qing Dynasty, the construction of the rule of law in the period of the 1911 Revolution, or the legal development in the period of the Beiyang Government of the Republic of China and the Nanjing National Government, during which a variety of constitutional models have emerged and various legal development models have been replaced, but none of them has really found the correct path to modernization of Chinese rule of law, Therefore, it is unlikely to promote the development and progress of Chinese society, or fundamentally change the tragic fate of the country and people. With the salvoes of Russia's October Revolution in 1917, Marxism-Leninism was brought to China. The May 4th Movement of 1919 spurred the spread of Marxism throughout the country. Since then, fundamental changes have taken place in Chinese society, and the CPC was born. The founding of the CPC in China was an epoch-making event, which profoundly changed the course of Chinese history in modern times, transformed the future of the Chinese people and nation, and altered the landscape of world development (Xi 2021a, b). Since the CPC stepped onto the stage of Chinese history for a century, in the great practice of promoting Chinese revolution, construction and reform, it has always attached importance to the construction of the rule of law, diligently explored its own path of development of rule of law and provided valuable historical experience for the formation of a new path of Chinese rule of law modernization.

First, accumulating practical experience for the establishment of a new political system. The history of human political development shows that the process of replacing the old political system with the new political system is often accompanied by fierce class struggle and social revolution. The new political system to be established by the proletarian revolution has the fundamental characteristics different from the previous political rule. It must be premised on breaking the old state machinery and establishing a new state power. In the great struggle of the new democratic revolution, the CPC, with Comrade *Mao Zedong* as their chief representative, combined the basic tenets of Marxism-Leninism with the actual practice of the Chinese revolution, opened up the correct revolutionary path of encircling cities in rural areas and seizing power with arms, created revolutionary bases in vast rural areas, established new democratic revolutionary power in some regions. While leading the people to carry out armed revolution, the CPC attaches great importance to the construction of people's political power, promulgates a series of constitutional documents, and establishes a people's democratic political power system suitable for different historical periods.

Secondly, further promoting the construction of the new democratic revolutionary legal system. In the great struggle of the new democratic revolution, Chinese Communists have a deep grasp of the development stage of the Chinese revolution and its legal requirements, adhere to Marxism-Leninism and Mao Zedong Thought as the guide for action, proceed from the specific reality of the Chinese revolution, and constantly promote the legal construction of the new democratic revolution under difficult circumstances, The establishment of a new legal system that is fundamentally opposed to the "Complete Book of Six Codes" system of the Nanjing National Government of the Republic of China has laid an important foundation for the rule of law to win the great victory of the new democratic revolution. On the whole, although the important legal principles and legal systems established by the new-democratic revolutionary legal system, such as the system of workers, peasants and soldiers' people's congress, the form of "the three-thirds principle" democratic political power, equality before the law, protection of human rights, freedom of marriage, equality between men and women, open trial, death penalty review, people's mediation system and so on, undoubtedly reflect the basic nature of the new legal system. Specifically, in addition to the above-mentioned constitutional documents issued and issued on behalf of the fundamental interests of the people, in different historical periods, the people's governments in the revolutionary base areas have launched a series of legislative activities according to the specific tasks of the new democratic revolution in each historical period.

Thirdly, striving to build a new democratic judicial system. In leading the people in the struggle for the new democratic revolution, the CPC attaches great importance to the construction of the judicial system, making it an important means to carry out the revolutionary struggle. In the framework of the judicial system, the judicial institutions should be established in accordance with the Soviet principle of the unity of legislative and executive powers. The Outline of the Constitution of the Soviet Republic of China stipulates that the National Soviet Congress and the Central Executive Committee have the power to formulate the systematic organization of the courts and promulgate civil, criminal and procedural laws; The Supreme Court was established under the Central Committee to ensure the effectiveness of the revolutionary laws of the Soviet Republic of China; Under the Soviet executive committees at the provincial, county, district and municipal levels, the judicial offices were established. The judicial system of the democratic regime in the border region during the war of resistance against Japanese aggression was also established in accordance with the principle of the unity of the executive and the executive. The administrative organs in the border region bear the responsibility of judicial adjudication. Even during the War of Liberation, the judicial system of combining justice and administration under the guidance of the principle of unity of law and practice still played a unique judicial role. In the long-term new democratic judicial practice, the judicial organs in the revolutionary base areas under the leadership of the CPC have kept in mind the fundamental purpose of justice for the people, adhered to the mass line, thoroughly done the mass work in judicial activities, properly resolved conflicts and disputes, earnestly safeguarded the most fundamental interests of the masses, and accumulated valuable judicial experience for China to promote the Chinese judicial modernization in the new era.

2.3 Preliminary Foundation of Chinese Rule of Law Path

The victory of the Chinese People's Revolution in 1949 and the founding of the People's Republic of China are one of the historic milestones in realizing the great rejuvenation of the Chinese nation since modern times, marking the country's great transformation from a millennia-old feudal autocracy to people's democracy. This also reshaped the world political landscape (Xi 2021a, b: 8). From the founding of the People's Republic of China to the decisive victory of the socialist transformation of private ownership of the means of production in 1956, this is the most profound and greatest period of social transformation in the history of thousands of years in China, and also the foundation period of the path of Chinese rule of law modernization.

The first is the creative building of a socialist national system with Chinese characteristics. With the victory of the Chinese People's Revolution throughout the country, the creation of a new political system, the realization of fundamental changes in the national system and governance system, and the opening up of a new path of Chinese rule of law modernization have become a serious and important historical task before the Chinese communists. The Chinese communists insist on starting from the basic national conditions of China, profoundly revealing the laws of the historical movement of the Chinese revolution and establishing the guiding principles for the development of the national system from the new democratic type to the socialist type. In the book "*On New Democracy*" (January 1940), *Mao Zedong* (1986: 351; 355) pointed out that the historical process of the Chinese revolution must be divided into two steps: the first step is the democratic revolution, and the second step is the socialist revolution, which are two revolutionary processes of different nature. The first step of the revolution is no longer the old revolution aimed at establishing the national system of the bourgeois dictatorship, but the new revolution aimed at establishing the national system of the joint dictatorship of all revolutionary classes, aiming at clearing a wider path for the development of socialism. In the book "*On the People's Democratic Dictatorship*" (June 30, 1949), *Mao Zedong* (1986: 687) incisively discussed the inevitability of establishing a people's democratic state power after the victory of China's New Democratic Revolution, pointing out that summing up our experience and focusing on this point is the people's democratic dictatorship led by the working class and based on the worker-peasant alliance. Under the guidance of the above theoretical principles, *The Common Programme* and *The Organic Law of the Central People's Government* adopted at the first plenary session of the Chinese People's Political Consultative Conference in September 1949 clearly stipulate the system of the new democratic state and its political power organization system at the beginning of the founding of New China, A new national system has been established. With the transition of China's society from new democracy to socialism, the first session of the first National People's Congress held in September 1954 adopted the Constitution of the People's Republic of China, which fixed the people's democracy and socialist principles in the form of the fundamental law of the country, and laid the fundamental law foundation for the comprehensive establishment of the socialist system in China. The "*May Fourth Constitution*" endows the nature of the country with new attributes and contents, stipulates that "the People's Republic of China is a people's democratic country led by the working class and based on the worker-peasant alliance" (Article 1), and summarizes the practical experience of democratic political construction since the founding of the People's Republic of China and the experience of the work of the organs of state power, makes more complete provisions on the fundamental political system of the country, and stresses that "all power in the People's Republic of China belongs to the people. The Organs through which the people exercise power are the National People's Congress and the local people's congresses." (Article 2). Thus, the people's congress system was formally established (Xi 2020: 67). It has further enriched the system of regional ethnic autonomy and improved the form of national structure, formed a civil rights system that is compatible with the nature and form of the national system, created the fundamental law foundation for the civil rights system of contemporary China, constructed a socialist national system and national governance system with Chinese characteristics, realized the historical transcendence of various national system programs since modern China, and created the constitutional basis for opening up a new path of Chinese rule of law modernization.

The second is the rebuilding of a new socialist legal order. In order to achieve its intended goal of social revolution, any violent social revolutionary movement should not only fundamentally change the nature and structure of the old national system and legal system, but also establish a new social and legal order on which the national system and legal system depend for existence and development. In a long historical period since the founding of the People's Republic of China, an obvious feature of Chinese rule of law modernization is that the development of rule of law and the mass movement are intertwined and form an organic interactive relationship. These large-scale mass movements have strongly promoted the development of the rule of law at the beginning of the founding of the People's Republic of China. Some laws were formulated after the mass movements. Under the social and historical conditions of the newly established regime of the People's Republic, launching mass movements and carrying out social reform is the basic way for our Party to organize social mobilization, rebuild social and legal order, and consolidate the new revolutionary regime. However, the revolutionary mass movement is not entirely dependent on the law, which may bring a by-product and encourage people to despise all legal systems, which also increases the difficulties for the Party and the country to overcome this mentality (Dong 2001: 350). Therefore, under the new historical condition that the country and social life have turned to economic construction as the center, the way to rely on mass movements to organize social mobilization, rebuild social and legal order, and promote national and social governance has become outdated. It is a must to formulate relatively complete laws systematically to promote the development of the country's rule of law and consolidate the legal basis of social order. The Eighth National Congress of the Communist Party of China, held in September 1956, based on the scientific analysis of the domestic and international situation since the founding of the People's Republic of China, made a major political judgment that the main contradiction facing Chinese society has been the contradiction between the people's requirements for the establishment of an advanced industrial country and the reality of a backward agricultural country, and the contradiction between the people's needs for the rapid development of economic and cultural and the current situation that economic and cultural cannot meet people's needs. Therefore, the Eighth National Congress of the Communist Party of China stressed that we shall further strengthen the people's democratic legal system and consolidate the order of socialist construction. The state must gradually and systematically formulate complete laws according to needs. All state organs and state functionaries must strictly abide by national laws, so that the people's democratic rights are fully protected by the state (China Institute of CPC Literature Research 2011: 301). This basic orientation of emphasizing and strengthening the construction of the rule of law is also reflected in the judicial field. Under the special social conditions at the beginning of the founding of the People's Republic of China, the judicial organs were included in the government system, and it was stipulated that the courts and procuratorates at the corresponding level should accept the leadership of the people's government committees at the same level and implement the judicial system of combining justice and administration, which has its historical rationality. With the continuous consolidation of the new people's political power and the gradual improvement of the national system, the principle and system of the independent exercise of powers by judicial organs according to law have been gradually established. The exploration of a new path to the modernization of Chinese rule of law increasingly shows a new historical trend.

The third is the launching of large-scale law-making activities. Under the complex social and historical conditions at the beginning of the founding of the People's Republic of China, liberating the social productive forces from the shackles of the old relations of production, consolidating the new revolutionary regime, and rebuilding the social and legal order can only, to a large extent, formulate some temporary laws with programmatic nature according to the policies of the Party and the people's government. At the beginning of the founding of the People's Republic of China, a prominent feature of exploring the new path of Chinese rule of law modernization is to promote national and social governance, not only by law, but also by policy. Policy adjustment plays a leading and dominant role in national and social governance. Nevertheless, the CPC still attaches importance to strengthening the people's democratic and legal construction and pays attention to governing the country and society by combining laws and policies, so as to meet the objective requirements of the continuous development of the new socio-economic and political situation. In the seven years from 1949 to the beginning of the founding of the People's Republic of China in 1956, the legal creation of the People's Republic of China has roughly experienced two successive stages of development. The first stage is the creation of laws based on *the Common Programme* with the nature of a provisional constitution, characterized by the use of legislative means to consolidate the victory of the People's Revolution and establish a new democratic political, economic, social and legal order to ensure the smooth progress of various social democratic reform movements. The second stage is to speed up the process of national legislation, promote the transformation from new democracy to socialism, comprehensively construct the legal basis of the socialist system, and promote the industrialization process of the country based on the "May Fourth Constitution". During this period, under the guidance of the "May Fourth Constitution", a number of important laws and decrees related to state organs and state systems were formulated. Especially in this period, the drafting of the civil law and criminal law of the People's Republic of China began to be put on the agenda. From the end of 1954, the Standing Committee of the First National People's Congress organized a special team to compile the Civil Code. By December 1956, the first draft of the Civil Code of the People's Republic of China was formed. It is clear that the legislative work in the early days of the founding of the People's Republic of China has indeed made important progress, gradually forming the framework of laws and regulations of the People's Republic of China with the "May Fourth Constitution" as the core, and making important progress in exploring the new path of Chinese rule of law modernization (Xi 2021a, b). In the process of exploring a new path of Chinese rule of law modernization, the original theoretical achievements of the CPC in the socialist revolution and construction and the important progress in the construction of the rule of law have provided valuable experience, theoretical preparation and practical basis for creating a new path of Chinese rule of law modernization in the new historical period of reform and opening up.

2.4 Formation of Chinese Rule of Law Path

The Third Plenary Session of the 11th CPC Central Committee, held in December 1978, launched a new great social revolution in contemporary China's reform and opening up, and Chinese rule of law modernization entered a new historical period of revolutionary change. Since the Third Plenary Session of the 11th CPC Central Committee, the CPC, as the ruling party, has always taken charge of the overall situation of this new great social revolution and led the movement direction of the new path of Chinese rule of law modernization, thoroughly summarized the successful experience and profound lessons of China's socialist rule of law construction, and put forward the major rule of law principles of socialist democracy institutionalization and legalization, We have made historic progress in Chinese rule of law modernization by defining the rule of law as the basic strategy for the Party to lead the people to govern the country and the rule of law as the basic way for the Party to govern the country.

First, the rule of law is established as the basic strategy of the CPC to lead the people in governing the country. The Third Plenary Session of the 11th CPC Central Committee seriously discussed the issue of democracy and the rule of law and put the historic task of strengthening the socialist rule of law and realizing the transformation from the rule of man to the rule of law before the whole party and the people, stressing that in order to guarantee people's democracy, it is necessary to strengthen the socialist legal system, institutionalize and legalize democracy, and make this system and law have stability, continuity and great authority, and put forward the rule of law construction policy in the new historical period that there are laws to go by, the laws are observed and strictly enforced, and law-breakers are prosecuted (China Institute of CPC Literature Research 1982: 10). The guidelines for the construction of the rule of law in China established at the Third Plenary Session of the 11th CPC Central Committee have strongly promoted the formation of a new path of Chinese rule of law modernization. The Second Session of the Standing Committee of the 5th NPC, held in July 1979, deliberated and passed seven laws, including the Criminal Law and the Criminal Procedure Law. In September 1979, the Central Committee of the Communist Party of China issued the Instruction on Firmly Ensuring the Effective Implementation of the Criminal Law and the Criminal Procedure Law to the whole party, which clearly put forward "the socialist rule of law" for the first time (China Institute of CPC Literature Research 2000:33), profoundly expounded the basic requirements of the work of the rule of law in criminal justice, and put whether the criminal law and the criminal procedure law can be strictly implemented to the important height "directly related to the credibility of the Party and the country", This is really significant and far-reaching. On December 4, 1982, the Constitution adopted at the fifth session of the Fifth National People's Congress (also known as "1982 Constitution Constitution") elevated the successful experience of our Party in promoting the rule of law since the Third Plenary Session of the CPC Central Committee to constitutional norms, established the principle of the unity of the country's legal system, and stipulated that "the country maintains the unity and dignity of the socialist legal system", so as to lay a solid foundation for the new path to the modernization of rule of law in China. Under the guidance of the "1982 Constitution", Chinese rule of law modernization is increasingly advancing in depth. The 15th National Congress of the Party held in September 1997, for the first time in the history of our Party, solemnly put forward the basic strategy of ruling the country in accordance with the law and building a socialist country of law, which is undoubtedly a historic strategic decision. The proposal and implementation of the basic strategy of law-based governance has injected new connotation into the new path of Chinese rule of law modernization and has effectively promoted the development process of the rule of law in contemporary China.

Second, law-based exercise of state power is defined as the basic way for the CPC to govern the country. The birth of New China has opened a new era in the history of the Chinese nation. The CPC has changed from the Party that leads the people in their struggle to seize national power to the Party that leads the people in their control of national power. With this huge and profound change, the CPC's ruling style is facing new major issues. In accordance with the guideline of "implementing the socialist rule of law", "September Directive" has, for the first time, comprehensively and scientifically established the basic principles and working mechanism of the CPC's leadership over judicial work, stressed the need to strengthen the Party's leadership over judicial work, and effectively ensured that judicial organs exercise the functions and powers stipulated in the Constitution and laws. In the future, the most important way to strengthen the leadership of the Party Committee on judicial work is to effectively ensure that the procuratorate exercises the procuratorial power independently and the court exercises judicial power independently, so that it will not be interfered by other administrative organs, groups and individuals. Based on the above understanding, "September Directive" announced that the Central Committee has decided to cancel the system of examining and approving cases by the Party committees (1982: 259) and put forward specific requirements for strengthening and improving the Party's leadership over judicial work under the new situation. "September Directive" has great political and legal significance, which has played an indispensable role in promoting the construction of the socialist judicial system with Chinese characteristics and the formation of a new path to the modernization of Chinese rule of law. Since the 1990s, the CPC Central Committee has repeatedly stressed the need to strengthen and improve the Party's leadership in the construction of the rule of law. Since the beginning of the twenty-first century, the CPC has profoundly revealed the ruling law of the Communist Party of China and made a major strategic deployment to reform and improve the Party's leadership and governance. The 16th National Congress of the CPC held in 2002 put forward the major proposition of ruling by law, pointing out that we shall enhance their awareness of law and know how to integrate the adherence to Party leadership and the people being the masters of the country with ruling the country by law and improve their abilities of exercising state power according to law (China Institute of CPC Literature Research 2002: 39). This is the fundamental guarantee for the CPC to lead the people to effectively govern the country and society under the new historical conditions. The Fourth Plenary Session of the 16th CPC Central Committee, held in September 2004, adopted the Decision of the CPC Central Committee on Strengthening the Construction of the Party's Governing Capacity, stressing that "law-based exercise of state power is a basic way for the Party to govern under the new historical conditions" (China Institute of CPC Literature Research 2006: 281). The proposal of the new ruling concept of law-based exercise of state power fully reflects the new requirements of the new social and historical conditions for the construction of the party's ruling ability. It is a major measure to strengthen and consolidate the ruling position of the CPC and promote the process of ruling the country by law, enriching and developing the basic content of the new path of Chinese rule of law modernization.

Third, the socialist legal system with Chinese characteristics under the leadership of the Constitution is formed and improved. With the historic development of the new path of Chinese rule of law modernization, the socialist legal system with Chinese characteristics is also gradually forming. The Third Plenary Session of the Eleventh Central Committee of the Communist Party of China clearly proposed that legislation should be placed on the important agenda of the national legislature from now on. Since then, following the important achievements and experience of the legislative development in the early days of the founding of the People's Republic of China, effectively strengthening the legislative work and gradually forming the socialist legal system with Chinese characteristics have become major events in promoting the process of the rule of law in the country and forming and developing a new path of Chinese rule of law modernization. The establishment of a legal system must be based on China's national conditions, proceed from China's actual conditions, and follow the path of the formation and development of a legal system with Chinese characteristics. Under the leadership of the Party Central Committee, the National People's Congress and its Standing Committee have launched the process of national legislation on a large scale. The socialist market economy is the law-based economy. After continuous exploration and practice, the 15th National Congress of the Communist Party of China put forward the fundamental principle of upholding the rule of law and at the same time clearly put forward the historic task of "accelerating the legislative work, improving the quality of legislation, and forming the socialist legal system with Chinese characteristics by 2010" for the first time. It is obvious that the specific timetable for the formation of a socialist legal system with Chinese characteristics has been set, which fully reflects the rational consciousness of contemporary CPC people to firmly open up a new path of Chinese rule of law modernization. Through the unremitting efforts since the founding of the People's Republic of China, especially since the new era of reform and opening up, the legislative cause of contemporary China has made great achievements. The current Constitution was formulated in 1982. Since then, according to the development needs of the objective situation, the National People's Congress has deliberated and adopted four amendments to the Constitution on April 12, 1988, March 28, 1993, March 15, 1999 and December 4, 2004, which profoundly reflects the interaction between constitutional system and social change. By the end of 2010, China has formulated 236 effective laws, 690 administrative regulations and more than 8600 local regulations, and has comprehensively completed the centralized cleaning of existing laws, administrative regulations and local regulations. At present, the legal departments covering all aspects of social life are complete, and the basic and major laws in all legal departments have been formulated, and the internal legal system is generally scientific and harmonious. Therefore, the fourth session of the 11th National People's Congress held in March 2011 solemnly announced that the socialist legal system with Chinese characteristics had been formed as scheduled, which is a great achievement (Xi 2020: 95) and is of great significance in the formation and development of the new path to modernization of Chinese rule of law.

2.5 Expansion of Chinese Rule of Law Path

Since the 18th National Congress of the CPC, the rule of law has become more prominent and important in the process of national modernization, and the new path of Chinese rule of law modernization has been further improved and expanded. Thus, it clearly shows the strategic vision and wisdom of improving and developing the new path of Chinese rule of law modernization.

First, putting forward the major strategic task of promoting the modernization of national governance and building a law-based China. The rule of law is an important symbol of the progress of human civilization and the institutional achievement of the development of social politics, economy and social civilization since modern times. In contemporary China, the rule of law is the basic way to govern the country and government. It aims to bring the country and social life into an institutionalized, standardized and procedural track and implement effective rule of law. The 18th National Congress of the CPC proposed to pay more attention to the important role of the rule of law in national governance and social management (China Institute of CPC Literature Research 2012: 24). The Third Plenary Session of the 18th Central Committee of the Communist Party of China defined improving and developing the socialist system with Chinese characteristics, promoting the modernization of the national governance system and governance capacity as the overall goal of comprehensively deepening reform, and recorded the historic task of promoting the rule of law in China in the Party's literature for the first time, stressing that to build a China under the rule of law, we must adhere to the rule of law, rule of law and administration in accordance with the law, and adhere to the integrated construction of a country under the rule of law, a government under the rule of law and a society under the rule of law (China Institute of CPC Literature Research 2013:31). The Fourth Plenary Session of the 18th CPC Central Committee was the first thematic study in the history of the CPC on several major issues concerning comprehensively promoting the rule of law, elaborately planning the strategic blueprint and overall layout for comprehensively promoting the rule of law, we solemnly call on all Party comrades and the people of all ethnic groups in the country to strive to build China into a rule of law country (China Institute of CPC Literature Research 2015: 6). The 19th National Congress of the Communist Party of China established "advancing overall law-based governance" as an organic component of the fundamental principle of adhering to and developing socialism with Chinese characteristics in the new era, emphasizing that advancing overall law-based governance is an essential requirement and important guarantee for socialism with Chinese characteristics; it is also a profound revolution in China's governance; it is a profound revolution in national governance (China Institute of CPC Literature Research 2017: 18; 31). The Second Plenary Session of the 19th Central Committee of the CPC deliberated and adopted the Proposal of the Central Committee of the CPC on Amending Part of the Constitution, which provides a strong constitutional guarantee for upholding and developing a society with Chinese characteristics in the new era. Accordingly, the first session of the 13th National People's Congress deliberated and adopted the fifth amendment to the current Constitution, enriched and improved the relevant provisions of the current Constitution, and clearly expressed the constitutional logic of the new path of Chinese rule of law modernization. The Third Plenary Session of the 19th CPC Central Committee made an important deployment to deepen the reform of the Party and state organs, and proposed that the party must accelerate the advancement of the modernization of the national governance system and governance capability and endeavor to form a more mature and better shaped socialist system with Chinese characteristics in order to better lead the people in carrying out the great struggle, building the great project, boosting the great cause, and realizing the great dream. That is a major task lying before the party (China Institute of CPC Literature Research 2018a: 14). According to the overall deployment of the 19th National Congress, it was decided to establish the Central Committee for the Comprehensive Rule of Law, in order to strengthen the centralized and unified leadership of the Central Committee of the Communist Party of China on the construction of the rule of law (China Institute of CPC Literature Research 2018b: 4). The Fourth Plenary Session of the 19th CPC Central Committee included upholding and improving the socialist rule of law system with Chinese characteristics and improving the Party's ability of law-based governance in the overall strategic deployment of promoting the construction of the national system and the national governance system, and put forward the specific tasks of strengthening the construction of the legal system in the new era (China Institute of CPC Literature Research 2019: 13–15). The Fifth Plenary Session of the 19th Central Committee of the Communist Party of China, starting from the reality that contemporary China has entered a new stage of development of building a socialist modern country in an all-round way, outlined the long-term goal of basically realizing the modernization of the rule of law by 2035, which is to basically build a country, a government and a society under the rule of law, and laid out the key tasks for the construction of the rule of law during the "Fourteenth Five-Year Plan" period. The Sixth Plenary Session of the 19th CPC Central Committee comprehensively summarized the great achievements and valuable experience of the CPC over the Past Century, and systematically reviewed the major progress made in the comprehensive rule of law since the 18th CPC National Congress, pointing out that since the 18th CPC National Congress, the socialist system of rule of law with Chinese characteristics has been continuously improved, the construction of China under the rule of law has taken solid steps, the role of the rule of law as a fundamental, stable and long-term guarantee has been further played, and the ability of the Party to lead and govern the country in the way of the rule of law has been significantly enhanced (China Institute of CPC Literature Research 2021: 43). Therefore, *Xi Jinping* (2020: 85) stressed that law is the important tool of governance, and the rule of law is an important support for the country's governance system and capacity. The new path of Chinese rule of law modernization is unfolding in a magnificent manner, profoundly changing the basic face of the country and social life.

The second is to clarify the overall objectives, strategic arrangements and key tasks of the comprehensive rule of law in the new era. In contemporary China, as the institutional basis and important support for the modernization of national governance, the overall rule of law has its own internal goal. The Fourth Plenary

Session of the 18th CPC Central Committee established "developing a rule of law system of socialism with Chinese characteristics and the rule of law in socialist China" as the overall goal of comprehensively promoting the rule of law, and stressed the need to establish a complete legal standard system, a highly efficient system for exercising the rule of law, a system for tight supervision of the rule of law, a system for powerful support for the rule of law, to form a perfect system of laws and regulations within the party (China Institute of CPC Literature Research 2014: 4). *Xi Jinping* (2020: 93) regards the construction of the socialist rule of law system with Chinese characteristics as the key approach to promoting the rule of law in an all-round way, and clearly required that all work of law-based governance should be planned and promoted around the key approach. Since the 18th National Congress of the Communist Party of China, the cause of rule of law, which concentrates on the construction of the socialist rule of law system with Chinese characteristics as the overall focus of the overall rule of law, has been carried out in depth, made significant steps and progress. The compilation and implementation of the Civil Code of the People's Republic of China is of great significance in the process of Chinese rule of law modernization in the new era. In the legislative history of the People's Republic of China, the Civil Code, the first law named after a code in New China, systematically integrates the civil legal norms formed in the long-term practice of the People's Republic of China over the past 70 years, and constructs a harmonious, coordinated, organic and unified civil legal system, with distinctive Chinese characteristics, practical characteristics, and characteristics of the times, and has a fundamental and important position in the socialist legal system with Chinese characteristics. It is of great significance and far-reaching significance for the building of a law-based China, developing a socialist market economy, safeguarding the legitimate rights and interests of the people, and promoting a new path of Chinese rule of law modernization. The 19th National Congress of the Communist Party of China, based on the new changes in the main contradictions of our society in the new era, made strategic arrangements for launching a new journey of comprehensively promoting the construction of a rule of law in China and realizing Chinese rule of law modernization, and determined a two-step road map and timetable for building a rule of law in China and realizing the modernization of national governance. That is, from 2020 to 2035, on the basis of building a moderately prosperous society in an all-round way, we will strive for another 15 years to basically realize the modernization of the country. In this process, the rule of law for the country, the government, and society is basically in place. Institutions in all fields are further improved; the modernization of China's system and capacity for governance is basically achieved; From 2035 to the middle of this century, on the basis of basically realizing national modernization, we will strive for another 15 years to build China into a great modern socialist country that is prosperous, powerful, democratic, civilized, harmonious, and beautiful, during which political civilization, including the civilization of the rule of law, will be comprehensively improved, and modernization of China's system and capacity for governance will be achieved (China Institute of CPC Literature Research 2017: 23). The strategic arrangement of the 19th National Congress on Chinese rule of law modernization in the new era clearly expresses the firm will of the contemporary

CPC to unswervingly adhere to and expand the new path of Chinese rule of law modernization. In his speech at the first meeting of the Central Committee for the Comprehensive Rule of Law, *Xi Jinping* (2020: 232–235) clarified seven key tasks, including researching and formulating the construction plan of law-based China, fully implementing the Constitution, further advancing the work of scientific legislation, strengthening the construction of law-based government, deepening the reform of judicial system, promoting the construction of law-based society and strengthening the construction of legal team and training of legal personnel. It is obvious that these strategic key tasks have effectively responded to the new requirements of the main contradictions and new changes in China's society in the new era for the construction of the rule of law in China, established the main direction of Chinese rule of law modernization in the new era, and will have a profound impact on adhering to and expanding the new path of Chinese rule of law modernization.

Third, the unity of advancing reforms under the rule of law and improving the rule of law in reforms shall be adhered to. In contemporary China, the process of Chinese rule of law modernization and the process of reform under the rule of law are intrinsically combined. Since the 18th CPC National Congress, the Party Central Committee with Comrade *Xi Jinping* as its core has carefully grasped the basic characteristics of China's national conditions for the rule of law. While drawing on and absorbing the beneficial achievements of the world's rule of law civilization, starting from China's reality, following the internal mechanism and laws of the modernization of Chinese rule of law, and adhering to the basic requirements of advancing reforms under the rule of law and improving the rule of law in reforms (Xi 2015: 52), it has embarked on an independent path of Chinese rule of law reform. The Third and Fourth Plenary Sessions of the 18th CPC Central Committee took comprehensively deepening reform and overall law-based governance as the theme and made decisions, which has close internal logic and is a sequence of overall deployment on the timeline, reflecting the dialectical unity of "breaking" and "establishing" (Xi 2015: 13–14). Reform and the rule of law are like two wings of a bird and two wheels of a car, which effectively promote the development of the new path of Chinese rule of law modernization. The reform of rule of law in China, which has entered the new era, focuses on strengthening the top-level design and overall planning, highlighting the systematism, integrity and synergy of the reform in the field of the rule of law, and strengthening the comprehensive consideration, mutual cooperation and overall coordination of the reform measures of the rule of law, so as to form a joint force, so as to make the reform plan of the rule of law more targeted, effective and operational. The reform of the rule of law in China, which has entered a new era, has focused on strengthening the problem orientation, seized the prominent and key issues in the work of the rule of law that are strongly reflected by the people and related to the overall situation of the construction of the rule of law. On the basis of in-depth investigation and research, it has launched strong measures for the reform of rule of law, overcome difficulties, forge ahead, and created a new situation in the reform of the rule of law. The reform of the rule of law in China, which has entered the new era, pays attention to enhancing the "sense of gain" of the people, adheres to the people-centered rule of law development criteria, takes the promotion and realization of social fairness and justice as the starting point and foothold of the reform of the rule of law, tests the success and failure of the reform of the rule of law by the people's satisfaction and "sense of gain", and strives to make the reform of the rule of law conform to the people's will and public opinion. The reform of the rule of law in China, which has entered the new era, attaches great importance to abiding by the principle of reform according to law, bringing the reform in the field of the rule of law into the orbit of the rule of law and promoting it, making great efforts to achieve the organic connection and mutual promotion of reform decision-making and legislative work, and adhering to the use of the rule of law to promote the reform in the field of the rule of law, so as to strive to solve the contradiction between the people's growing new need for the rule of law and the unbalanced and inadequate development of the rule of law, and to open up a new realm of Chinese rule of law path.

2.6 Conclusion

The unique national conditions and cultural traditions determine that China must follow a modern rule of law path suitable for its own characteristics. We shall follow our own path—this is the historical conclusion our Party has drawn from its endeavors over the past century (The CPC Central Committee 2021: 67). Since the founding of the CPC, the CPC has united and led the people to carry out a great social revolution of great hardship and grandeur, combined the basic principles of the Marxist theory on the rule of law with China's specific reality, and with China's excellent traditional legal culture, adhered to the national conditions and independently explored and formed a new path of Chinese rule of law modernization in line with the national conditions, which is of great significance in the process of world rule of law modernization.

References

China Institute of CPC Literature Research. 2000. *Collection of documents of the 15th national congress of the CPC.* People's Publishing House.

China Institute of CPC Literature Research. 2002. *Collection of Documents of the 16th National Congress of the CPC.* People's Publishing House.

China Institute of CPC Literature Research. 2006. *Selected Important Documents Since the 16th National Congress II.* Central Party Literature Press.

China Institute of CPC Literature Research. 2011. *Selected important documents since the founding of the People's Republic of China.* Central Party Literature Press.

China Institute of CPC Literature Research. 2012. *Collection of Documents of the Eighteenth National Congress of the Communist Party of China.* People's Publishing House.

China Institute of CPC Literature Research. 2013. *Decision of the Central Committee of the Communist Party of China on several major issues concerning comprehensively deepening reform.* People's Publishing House.

China Institute of CPC Literature Research. 2014. *Decision of the Central Committee of the Communist Party of China on several major issues concerning comprehensively promoting the rule of law.* People's Publishing House.

China Institute of CPC Literature Research. 2015. *Proposal of the Central Committee of the Communist Party of China on formulating the 13th five year plan for national economic and social development.* People's Publishing House.

China Institute of CPC Literature Research. 2017. *Collection of Documents of the 19th National Congress of the Communist Party of China.* People's Publishing House.

China Institute of CPC Literature Research. 2018a. *Decision of the Central Committee of the Communist Party of China on deepening the reform of the Party and State institutions.* People's Publishing House.

China Institute of CPC Literature Research. 2018b. *Deepening the reform plan of the Party and State institutions.* People's Publishing House.

China Institute of CPC Literature Research. 2019. *Decision of the Central Committee of the Communist Party of China on several major issues concerning adhering to and improving the socialist system with Chinese characteristics and promoting modernization of the national governance system and capacity.* People's Publishing House.

Dong, B. 2001. *Dong Biwu's collected works on law.* Law Press.

Mao, Z. 1986. *Selected readings of Mao Zedong's Works*, vol. I. People's Publishing House.

The Communist Party of China (CPC) Central Committee. 2021. *Resolution of the Central Committee of the Communist Party of China on the major achievements and historical experience of the Party over the past century.* People's Publishing House.

Xi, J. 2015. *Excerpts from Xi Jinping's discussion on law-based governance in all fields.* Central Party Literature Press.

Xi, J. 2017. *Compilation of Documents of the 19th National Congress of the CPC.* People's Publishing House.

Xi, J. 2020. *On adhering to overall law-based governance of China.* Central Party Literature Press.

Xi, J. 2021a. Speech at a ceremony marking the centenary of the Communist Party of China. *People's Daily*, July 2.

Xi, J. 2021b. Unswervingly follow the path of socialist rule of law with Chinese characteristics to provide strong legal guarantee for the comprehensive construction of a modern socialist country. *Qiushi* 5.

Chapter 3
Cultural Resources of Chinese Rule of Law Path

Abstract The cultural resources of Chinese rule of law path signify the necessary reliance on the excellent traditional legal system resources and legal cultural resources of China, as well as the valuable explorations and lessons learned from modern legal practices, in order to promote the innovative development of the Chinese rule of law modernization in the new era. The Chinese legal system embodies the spirit and wisdom of the Chinese nation, with many excellent ideas and concepts that are worth inheriting. These include the national governance strategy of making ritual and rite violations criminal offenses and valuing rites and laws; the concept that the people are the foundation of a nation, and a nation can enjoy peace only when its foundation is strong; the value that the country should be free from litigation and harmony is precious; the idea of "prudent punishment", the idea of prioritizing virtues over sanctions; the equality concept of making sanctions appropriate to the crime in accordance with the law and the principle of protecting those who have no kin and cannot support themselves as well as the elderly, minors, women, and those with disabilities. All these show the wisdom of the excellent Chinese traditional legal culture.

3.1 Introduction

Standing at the "historical convergence period" of the "two Centenary" Goals, Chinese modernization path presents new characteristics of the times: that is, innovative modernization that attaches importance to innovative thinking (Ma 2021: 26). The new modernization in the new era will take the new development concept as its essence and realize the comprehensive transformation from concept to system. In this sense, relying on excellent historical resources and guided by the advanced concept of innovative development, endowing historical resources with innovative interpretation and creative transformation is indispensable to the steady construction of Chinese modernization path. The establishment of a new path of Chinese rule of law modernization is a creative transformation of modernization based on the excellent gene of the excellent traditional Chinese legal civilization, which is full of

© The Author(s), under exclusive license to Springer Nature Singapore Pte Ltd. 2024
X. Dong and J. Guo, *Chinese Rule of Law Path and Cultivation of Foreign-Related Rule of Law Talents*, https://doi.org/10.1007/978-981-97-2313-3_3

the profound connotation of the modern transformation of the traditional rule of law civilization. The new path of Chinese rule of law modernization should undoubtedly be based on the rich historical resources of Chinese traditional legal culture. We need to attach importance to these historical resources and creatively transform them so that they can provide firm cultural resources for the great journey of building a new path of Chinese rule of law modernization and accumulate energy for Chinese rule of law to stand rock-firm in the in the rule of law world. Only by making a historical review and academic summary of it can we refine the excellent historical factors, and find the connection point with modern society, thus casting the great historical journey of rule of law modernization with Chinese characteristics.

3.2 Cultural Resources of Chinese Rule of Law Path

Marx and Engels (2009: 12) pointed out with great insight that the degree of realization of a theory in a country always depends on the degree to which the theory meets the needs of the country. Chinese political system, which has lasted for thousands of years since ancient times, has its profound ideological and cultural foundation. In the process of the formation and creation of the system, it is also built on the basis of ideological and cultural resources. These important ideological and cultural resources nourish the great journey of the new path of Chinese rule of law modernization, and constantly inject theoretical nutrients into it.

1. Ideal of the Grand Union

The ideal of the Grand Union is an ideal world where the Great Way rules for the common good. Confucianism in the pre-Qin period gave birth to the ideal of Grand Union. As stated in *The Book of Rites,* when the grand course was pursued, a public and common spirit ruled all under the sky; they chose men of talents, virtue, and ability; their words were sincere, and what they cultivated was harmony. Thus, mend did not love their parents only, nor treat as children only their own sons. A competent provision was secured for the aged till their death, employment for the able-bodied, and the means of growing up to the young. They showed kindness and compassion to widows, orphans, childless men, and those who were disabled by disease, so that they were all sufficiently maintained. Males had their proper work, and females had their homes. (They accumulated) articles (of value), dislike that they should be thrown away upon the ground, but not wishing to keep them for their own gratification. (They labored) with their strength, disliking that it should not be exerted, but not exerting it (only) with a view to their own advantage. In this way (selfish) scheming were repressed and found no development. Robbers, filchers, and rebellious traitors did not show themselves, and hence the outer doors remained open, and were not shut. This was (the period of) what we call the Grand Union. As the key words entrusted to *Confucius*, its original intention is to criticize and reflect on the vision that the grand course has fallen into disuse and obscurity, and the kingdom is a family inheritance, thus depicting an ideal picture of the Grand Union, in order to form a stark contrast between the ancient and modern. This imaginative picture undoubtedly contains the desire of pre-Qin philosophers for the sound operation of social order based on "rites". The "rites" constructed since the Western Zhou Dynasty actually played a role in maintaining the good order of social stability in the traditional society. As far as "a public and common spirit ruled all under heaven" is concerned, the realization of the Grand Union in the world is based on the harmonious order created by the united efforts of the world. In modern times, Kang (1987: 240) put more emphasis on the combination of "the common good will reign over all under Heaven" and the idea of equality, and put forward the proposition that everyone is public, everyone is equal, so we can be in great harmony with others. The "Three People's Principles" advocated by Sun (2011: 191), which are the government of the people, by the people, for the people, are intended to truly achieve the Grand Union that *Confucius* hoped for, which undoubtedly provides a more comprehensive value goal for the Grand Union.

2. Unified Tradition of the Whole Country

The unified tradition of the world is a shared value by all the people and united country of all the people. Qin united the six countries, and then strengthened the centralization of power with strong legal measures. Through the construction of "vehicles on the same track, books on the same text" and weights and measures, the people's understanding of unification was strengthened, and the system shaped the traditional constitutional pattern of historical China (Zhu 2017), reflecting the unified tradition of "shared values by all the people and united country of all the people". Since the Qin and Han dynasties, the political system containing many civilizations has become the norm in Chinese history. "Unity of the Whole Country" has become the feature of the structure of Chinese feudal society and the honor and pride of the Chinese nation. Based on this, the "super stable structure" of traditional society has been formed (Jin and Liu 2010: 21). After *Dong Zhongshu*'s policy of "rejecting the other schools of thought and respecting only Confucianism", the ideology with Confucianism as the core wrapped the centralized system created by Qin, thus providing more practical institutional and ideological support for this great tradition. Thus, as a unified entity structure that integrates geographical territory and political and economic orientation, it is also endowed with cultural attributes and ideology, and finally integrated into the historical process of the Chinese nation. In the historical reality of "unification" and "division", it has always maintained the theme of "division" to "unification". In this sense, the tradition of "Unity of the Whole Country" is full of the national orientation of pursuing unity and opposing division, a series of central political arrangements aimed at forming cohesion, and a worldly orientation of a resilient and flexible cultural and educational system (Ren 2021: 88). In this sense, it has key value for the construction of social order, political system, the shaping of national consciousness, and even the formation of civilization and cultural characteristics.

3. The Diplomatic Way

The diplomatic way is based on the principles of good neighborliness and harmony in relations with all other countries. Traditional China, with its precocious and spontaneous political literacy, has properly handled the good-neighborly and friendly relations with the surrounding areas, and gradually formed a supranational civilization system, a super-stable multi-ethnic country, and a political civilization that radiates neighboring countries and regions in the course of thousands of years of history. It is the most important to reach benevolence and righteousness and make friendship with the neighboring states (Zuo 2017: 11), which has gradually become the creed to be followed when dealing with the relations between states. In the shaping of this civilization, the unified Chinese nation upholds the primary value and basic concept of "harmony", advocates harmony, peaceful coexistence, and recognizes and respects diversity. It also focuses on the tolerance and respect of its own people and tries to mediate disputes with the mentality of peace, harmony and cooperation. It also effectively regulates the internal social order through moral education, Confucian ethics and policy coordination, so as to achieve long-term stability of national governance. In the founding of such unification, "harmony among nations" has become the highest goal. The realization of this process is not based on foreign conquest, but on the stability of domestic politics, the outward penetration of the Central Plains civilization and the great integration of national cultures. In this process, the initial model of China's foreign relations has undoubtedly formed.

4. The Proposition of Rule of Virtue

The proposition of rule of virtue means putting morality first and punishment subsidiary, publicity of moral power and cautious application of punishment. Similar to the concept of "rule of law", the concept of "rule of virtue" was initiated by legalists. Before the emergence of "rule of virtue" as a concept, "rule of virtue" existed long ago, and its traces can be found in classic works such as the *Book of Poetry* or *Shang Shu.* At that time, the rulers were required to comply with the natural principles and implement benevolent policies with respect for virtue and enlightened virtue. Then the "moral policy", which is derived from it, has more clearly popularized the theory of "moral policy for politics" and has become the rule of governance advocated by Confucianism. Among them, it is mixed with the emphasis on the moral education of the people: if you guide the people with ordinances and statutes and keep them in line with threats of punishment, they will try to stay out of trouble but will have no sense of shame. If you guide them with exemplary virtue and keep them in line with the practice of the rites, they will have a sense of shame and will know to reform themselves. From the transformation of virtue to moral governance, it can be seen that the essence of Confucian virtue is to take self-discipline norms as its main content, and the object of its norms is not the ordinary people, but the rulers. It can be found that what virtue pursues is to start from his own heart, grow through continuous cultivation, and finally promote his inner cultivation to the outside world. In addition, from the perspective of function, virtue does not exist in isolation, but needs to play its fundamental role through the combination of punishment and etiquette. The rule of virtue of Chinese traditional Confucianism is a strategy of ruling the country with virtue as the main principle and punishment as the auxiliary. It not only advocates the internal normative role of morality, but also does not ignore the external punishment role of punishment. Both of them serve together to maintain the stability of social order in a primary and secondary way, with moral education as the main and punishment as the auxiliary.

5. The Concept that People are the Foundation of a State

The concept that people are the foundation of a state is a typical representative of China's excellent political culture since ancient times. As early as the Western Zhou Dynasty, the rulers had a deep understanding of the governance concept of respecting the heaven and protecting the people. The ideological origin of "valuing the people" is presented in *Shangshu*: our great ancestor remains the instruction so bright, we should be kind to the people and never think of them in light; the people are the root of the nation, if the root is tight, the nation will be peaceful. It can be regarded as the earliest appeal of the concept that people are the foundation of the society. Since the Spring and Autumn Period, the concept that people are the foundation of a state has been in the ascendant. Political thinkers such as *Guan Zhong* and *Yan Zi* have expressed their early opinion that whoever wishes to put his state in order must value the common people of his state. During the Warring States Period, Confucian thinkers focused on this, and especially the idea advocated by *Mencius* that in a state the people are the first element, land and grain are the next and the least is the sovereign has become the most famous saying of the concept that people are the foundation of a state. *Mencius*'s words are based on the theory of benevolent government, while *Xunzi* emphasized the importance of the concept that people are the foundation of a state from the perspective of "equal emphasis on rites and law". Although their philosophical positions are different, they are ultimately implemented in the theoretical proposition of the concept that people are the foundation of a state. In short, the concept shows the distinctive characteristics of the traditional Chinese political governance, such as attaching importance to the people and caring about the people's livelihood, which has greatly affected the final casting of the basic idea of people-centered governance since modern times.

6. The Concept of Equality

Traditional Chinese people's understanding of the concept of equality is mostly taken from the word "equality". As early as in the *Book of Change*, there has been a record of the concept of equality. The junzi should follow its spirit to decrease what is excessive and to increase what is short of, and measure thing in an equal way. The change of times is not enough to dispel the root of this concept of equality in China, but also to gradually form the idea that the head of a state and the head of a hereditary family should not worry about poverty but should worry about inequity in the distribution of wealth and they should not worry about a lack of population but should worry about discontentment and unrest, which ultimately became the values of the Chinese nation. Both the rulers of all dynasties and the general public recognized the legitimacy of the Chinese concept of equality. In particular, *Confucius*, the representative of Confucianism, explained this concept of equality in great detail and depth. *Confucius* said, when there is equity in the distribution of wealth, there will not be poverty. When there is concordance in a society, there will not be a lack of population. When people are content, there will not be any threat of the state or the family being toppled. According to *Confucius*, there are differences between people in identity, endowment, ability, degree of diligence and other aspects, so the resources occupied and income obtained can also be different. But this difference between people must be kept within a reasonable limit, neither absolutely average nor absolutely wide (Han 2016). Therefore, the traditional Confucian concept of equality is not an absolute elimination of the gap between the rich and the poor, but rather a proper consideration of the interests of all social strata in order to achieve a balance in economic interests.

7. The Pursuit of Justice

The pursuit of the ultimate ideal of justice is the common belief of Chinese and Western societies, and the way to achieve justice shows the wisdom of Chinese and Western thinkers. When it comes to the realization of a certain degree of justice by law, the legalist thought of the Spring and Autumn and Warring States Period should be emphasized. *Yan Zi* said, when they applied punishments, they did not shy away from the nobles, and when they gave rewards, they did not neglect the lowly, which means that the law is the standard of social governance and the law and the illegal are rewarded and punished; As far as *Han Feizi* is concerned, he has given full play to the attribute of law as a tool of national governance. The most typical expression is that the law does not fawn on the noble; the string does not yield to the crooked. The law does not fawn on the noble, which means that the law does not distinguish between high and low, and treats the same as benevolence, and emphasizes that the legalists advocate equal punishment. The string does not yield to the crooked, which emphasizes that the law should uphold the standard of justice and should not tilt to the bend, which means that the law must become the standard to measure the right and wrong in social disputes. Compared with the legalists' pursuit of fairness, Confucianism pays more attention to moral ethics. Confucianism attaches importance to nobleness, inferiority, seniority, and familiarity, and advocate fathers cover up for their sons, and sons cover up for their fathers. To inherit and carry forward the traditional spirit of rule of law, the pursuit of justice reflected by the concept that the law does not fawn on the noble and the string does not yield to the crooked, it is necessary to establish the concept of rule of law that the constitution and the law are supreme and everyone is equal before the law, and put the spirit of rule of law through the whole process of legislation, law enforcement, justice, and law-abiding.

8. The Moral Integrity

The moral integrity is featured by filial piety, loyalty, integrity and honesty. The traditional Chinese model of rule of rite contains the dual connotations of "礼(li)" and "law". The elements of individual moral connotation, social ethical norms and public rationality in the patriarchal relationship network contained in the legacy of rule of etiquette still have certain reference value for the current modernization of China's national governance and even the new path of Chinese rule of law modernization. As a traditional Chinese model of state governance, the rule of rite imposes different moral constraints on the rulers and the commoners who are governed. As far as the rulers are concerned, since the Western Zhou Dynasty began to construct the special meaning of "virtue" and governance, virtue is expressed as a constraint on the rulers, requiring them to respect the heaven, respect the ancestors, and protect the people. In other words, it means to follow the heavenly mandate, respect the teachings of the Heavenly Emperor and ancestors, care for the people of the world, and be a ruler with virtue and moral principles. As for the ruled commoners, *Mencius* believes in affection between father and son, righteousness between sovereign and subject, attention to their different functions between husband and wife, the proper order between old and young, and honesty between friends, pointing out the direction for individual moral requirements and ethical relationship norms under different social roles. As a result, through the transformation by the Confucian scholars in the pre-Qin period, "礼" (li) shifted from expressing fear, supplication, and obedience towards mysterious nature and spirits to emphasizing the importance of human beings themselves. It extended to encompass the respect for and maintenance of human relationships and social order, with ethical guidelines for the five basic relationships of ruler and subject, father and son, husband and wife, elder and younger, and friends becoming the main content of "礼" (li). With this, a hierarchical order based on "礼"(li) was established, becoming a fundamental principle for governing the country.

9. The Spirit of Reform

The state of Zhou is old and receives the order from heaven. This dynasty has a bright future given by the god. The initial meaning expressed is that although the state established by the Zhou people is ancient, its divine mission lies in innovation. The saying is extended to express mission of the ancient country of China is to renew, and through reform, it will continuously glow with new vitality. This reform and innovation spirit has rich connotation. That is to say, reform and innovation are the excellent traditions of the Chinese nation since ancient times. In *the Book of Change*, there has been a saying that when there is no way to go, change will take place; change will be unobstructed and then it will continue long. Its core meaning is to emphasize the importance of change. The traditional Chinese culture under the traditional Confucian concept upholds the thought and spirit of reform and innovation. Historical experience tells us that reform is not achieved overnight, and the hardships and iterations are long-term. How to deal with this situation, first of all, we need to make corresponding changes as the world changes. We can neither copy what the ancients did, nor stick to the rules, but take corresponding measures according to the specific situation at that time. Secondly, the reform should also adapt to the times and grasp the opportunity to make judgments and choices that are suitable for the needs of the times. It includes conforming to the natural course of things and doing our utmost within human capabilities. The natural course of things keeps evolving, and human affairs should also keep pace with the times.

10. The Concept of Peace

Peace is the most important and that belligerent will perish. As far as foreign relations are concerned, traditional China firmly believes in the concept of peace, which values peace and is belligerent and doomed to death. This concept has its theoretical origin, which is the rule of rite order full of benevolence. To a large extent, this order is to transcend the national level and view the world from the perspective of the world. From this point of view, the "benevolence and justice" emphasized by Confucianism is not only a moral principle, but also a concept of governance. Some scholars call it the moral gold rule (Zhao 2005). In the eyes of the Confucians, this principle is contained in the internal governance of the country and the diplomatic level with other countries. For the former, it means that the king cares about his subjects and people, while the latter requires peaceful coexistence with neighboring countries and non-interference in the internal affairs of other countries. This kind of thought is a simple idea of harmony between people, mutual respect, and equality between countries. This is the Confucian ideal of the world social order, which has established a high degree of authority in the spiritual life of the Chinese nation. Since the unification of the Qin and Han dynasties to form a centralized state, the Chinese culture has been Confucian while accommodating other civilizations, thus contributing to the stability and development of the Chinese nation for more than 2000 years. In terms of diplomatic strategy, China strives to be inclusive of countries and regions with different systems and economic levels. This inclusiveness demonstrates magnanimity and a sense of being a great country, respecting the diversity of others and understanding their diverse perspectives.

3.3 Conclusion

Unlike civil law, common law, and Islamic law, Chinese law was formed under specific historical conditions in China, demonstrating the great creativity of the Chinese nation and the profound foundation of Chinese legal culture. Chinese legal system embodies the spirit and wisdom of the Chinese nation, with many excellent ideas and concepts that are worth inheriting. These include the national governance strategy of making ritual and rite violations criminal offenses and valuing rites and laws; the concept that the people are the foundation of a nation, and a nation can enjoy peace only when its foundation is strong; the value that the country should be free from litigation and harmony is precious; the idea of "prudent punishment", the idea of prioritizing virtues over sanctions; the equality concept of making sanctions appropriate to the crime in accordance with the law and the principle of protecting those who have no kin and cannot support themselves as well as the elderly, minors, women, and those with disabilities. All these show the wisdom of the excellent Chinese traditional legal culture. To explore a new path of Chinese rule of law modernization, we must thoroughly study the Chinese legal civilization tradition, excavate and inherit the essence of the Chinese traditional legal culture, draw nutrition from it, select the good and use it, and strive to promote the creative transformation and innovative development of the Chinese excellent legal civilization tradition. How to make the Chinese traditional legal culture thoughts and systems glow in the current casting of the modernization of the rule of law undoubtedly needs to be based on the present and strive to explore the modern factors of the traditional legal culture thoughts and systems, so as to complete the modern transformation, and jointly contribute to the great journey of the new path of Chinese rule of law modernization.

References

Han, T. 2016. The middle way concept of confucius thought on equalization distribution. *Confucius Studies* 4: 34–40.

Jin, G., and Liu, Q. 2010. *The cycle of growth and decline on the ultrastable structure of Chinese society*. Law Press.

Kang, Y. 1987. *Selected academic works of Kang Youwei*. Chinese Publishing House.

Ma, M. 2021. The historical evolution and prospect of the new path to Chinese modernization. *Historical Research* 6: 21–29.

Marx, K., and Engels, F. 2009. *Collected works of Marx and Engels*, vol. 1. People's Publishing House.

Ren, F. 2021. Great unification and the fundamental issues of political order: theoretical enlightenment of Qian Mu's historical thinking. *The Journal of Humanities*, 8, 80–89. https://doi.org/10.15895/j.cnki.rwzz.2021.08.009

Sun, Y. 2011. *Three people's principles of China*. China Chang'an Publishing House.

Zhao, T. 2005. On the best possible solution to the golden rule. *China Social Sciences* 3: 70–79.

Zhu, S. 2017. On the institutional significance of uniform weights and measures in historical China. *Science of Law (Journal of Northwest University of Political Science and Law)*, 1, 26–39. https://doi.org/10.16290/j.cnki.1674-5205.2017.01.003

Zuo, Q. 2017. *Zuo Zhuan the Annals of Lu's History from 722 to 468 BC. translated by Luo Zhiye*. Southeast University Press.

Chapter 4
Overall Objectives of Chinese Rule of Law Path

Abstract The overall goal of Chinese rule of law path is to provide a correct direction for China's overall law-based governance in the new era. The achievement of the overall goal of Chinese rule of law path requires adhering to the leadership of the Communist Party, putting people at the center, ensuring equality before the law, integrating the rule of law with the rule of virtue, taking into account China's actual conditions, promoting sound lawmaking, strict law enforcement, impartial administration of justice, and the observance of law by everyone, pursuing coordinated progress in law -based governance, law-based exercise of state power, and law-based government administration, and promoting the integrated development of rule of law for the country, the government, and society.

4.1 Introduction

Chinese rule of law modernization must take the right path and set clear objectives in order to utilize various parties and reap long-term benefits. The overall objectives of the path of Chinese rule of law modernization point out the correct direction for the overall law-based governance of the country in the new era. On the basis of the objectives, we shall unswervingly adhere to the nature and direction of the new path to modernization of the rule of law with Chinese characteristics, and unswervingly adhere to the socialist rule of law with Chinese characteristics. The determination of the overall objectives of the path of Chinese rule of law modernization should be based on a profound summary of the successful experience and historical achievements in the construction of the rule of law, and a more regular and creative scientific summary should be made.

Since the 18th CPC National Congress, the CPC Central Committee with Comrade *Xi Jinping* as the core has positioned, laid out, and implemented the rule of law from the strategic overall height of the future and destiny of the Party and the country, integrating the overall law-based governance of the country into the Chinese dream of realizing the great rejuvenation of the Chinese nation, into the huge systematic project of coordinated advancement of the five-sphere integrated plan including economic,

© The Author(s), under exclusive license to Springer Nature Singapore Pte Ltd. 2024
X. Dong and J. Guo, *Chinese Rule of Law Path and Cultivation of Foreign-Related Rule of Law Talents*, https://doi.org/10.1007/978-981-97-2313-3_4

political, cultural, social, and ecological progress and the Four-Pronged Comprehensive Strategy (that is, coordinate efforts to build a modern socialist country in all respects, comprehensively deepen reform, fully advance the law-based governance of China, and strengthen Party self-governance in every respect) into the framework of the modernization of the governance capacity of the national governance system. Comprehensive and effective exploration and practice have been made from the perspective of connection between history and reality, correlation between international and domestic laws, and the combination of theory and practices centering on a series of major issues such as why and how to achieve the overall law-based governance of the country in the new era, and great achievements in the construction of the rule of law have been obtained. A profound understanding and comprehensive grasp of the rich connotation of the overall objectives of Chinese rule of law modernization not only provides a correct and clear direction for the establishment of the overall layout of the new road, but also indicates that we should grasp the overall objectives from the overall development of the Party and the country's cause, plan for development, and constantly promote the development process of the path of Chinese rule of law modernization.

4.2 Chinese Rule of Law Modernization and Realization of the Great Rejuvenation of the Chinese Nation

Realizing the great rejuvenation of the Chinese nation is the political declaration of the Party and the country for the future. It focuses on upholding and developing socialism with Chinese characteristics, and embodies the historical responsibility and mission pursued by the CPC. The realistic basis for realizing the great rejuvenation of the Chinese nation is to achieve the "Two Centenary Goals". In accordance with the spirit of the 19th CPC National Congress, by the time the CPC is founded 100 years ago, we will have built a moderately prosperous society in all respects, and by the 100 years since the founding of the People's Republic of China, a great modern socialist country that is prosperous, powerful, democratic, culturally advanced, harmonious, and beautiful will have been built. The "Two Centenary Goals" are actually the embodiment of the great rejuvenation of the Chinese nation in the new era. The great rejuvenation of the Chinese nation represents the unremitting efforts of countless people with lofty ideals and is the unswerving belief of all Chinese people.

1. The Dream of the Great Rejuvenation of the Chinese Nation and "Four Greatness"

The realization of the great rejuvenation of the Chinese nation is premised on the achievement of national independence and people's liberation as well as national prosperity and common prosperity of the people. This great struggle, great project, great cause, and great dream are closely connected, flow seamlessly into each other, and are mutually reinforcing (Xi 2017a, b). To realize our great dream—the Chinese

Dream of national rejuvenation, we shall combine the practice of carrying out the great struggle, building the great project, and boosting the great cause.

Realizing our great dream demands a great struggle. To realize the great dream of national rejuvenation, we shall effectively respond to major challenges, withstand major risks, overcome major obstacles, and address major conflicts, and undertake a great struggle with many new contemporary features. All thinking and behavior in the vein of pleasure seeking, inaction and sloth, and problem avoidance are unacceptable. We shall more consciously uphold Party leadership and the system of socialism with Chinese characteristics; resolutely oppose all statements and actions that undermine, distort, or negate the Chinese socialist system; firmly oppose all moves that damage their interests or put distance between the Party and the people; firmly safeguard China's sovereignty, security, and development interests, and staunchly oppose all attempts to split China or undermine its ethnic unity and social harmony and stability; and be ready to fight, build our ability, and keep striving to secure new victories in this great struggle.

Realizing our great dream demands a great project. This project is the great new project of Party building that is just getting into full swing. As history has shown and will continue to bear witness to, without the leadership of the Communist Party of China, national rejuvenation would be just wishful thinking (Xi 2017a, b). As the vanguard of the times, the backbone of the nation, and the Marxist governing party, the CPC has and will always have the courage to face problems squarely, act to remove whatever undermines the Party's purity and advanced nature, keep on strengthening the Party's ability to lead politically, to guide through theory, to organize the people, and to inspire society, thus ensuring that the smooth implementation of the great new project of Party building.

Realizing our great dream demands a great cause. Socialism with Chinese characteristics has been a great cause for the benefit of the Chinese people, the focus of all of the Party's theories and practice since reform and opening up began, the product of the combination of the basic principles of Marxism with China's reality and the characteristics of the times. Since the reform and opening up, we have always held high the great banner of socialism with Chinese characteristics, constantly promoted the all-round development of people, and the people's sense of fulfillment, happiness, and security has increased day by day. To this end, in the new era, we need to consciously enhance our confidence in the path, theory, system and culture, adhere to the principle of doing things to prosper the country, do the good solid work that sees our country thrive, and continue to uphold and develop socialism with Chinese characteristics.

2. "Four Greatness" Cannot be Separated from the Realization of the Overall Objectives of Chinese Rule of Law Modernization

Realizing the Chinese dream of the great rejuvenation of the Chinese nation is of great strategic significance to the modernization of national governance system and capacity, and to the overall improvement of the Party's governance capacity; At the same time, building a socialist rule of law system with Chinese characteristics and a socialist rule of law China, the overall goal of comprehensively promoting the rule of law, is also one of the major strategic goals of realizing the Chinese dream of the great rejuvenation of the Chinese nation. The great rejuvenation of the Chinese nation is inseparable from the dream of the rule of law. To realize the Chinese dream of the great rejuvenation of the Chinese nation, we must comprehensively promote the rule of law (Xi 2014).

First of all, the realization of the great rejuvenation of the Chinese nation needs the scientific decision-making of the party and government institutions, the effective protection of the people's rights and interests, and the long-term stability of the country and social order, which can only be presented under the rule of law system and order. We shall raise the path of Chinese rule of law modernization to the new height of the overall development strategy of realizing the great rejuvenation of the Chinese nation and carry forward the spirit of the rule of law and cultivate the culture of the rule of law into the Chinese dream of the great rejuvenation of the Chinese nation. We shall further promote the standardization and institutionalization of various undertakings and projects through the rule of law, strengthen the legitimacy foundation of the construction of various undertakings and mechanisms, safeguard the legitimate rights of various social subjects in the realization of the great dream through the rule of law, and provide all-round institutional guarantee for the realization of a socialist modern power.

Secondly, the world and national conditions show that there are many opportunities and challenges in the path of achieving the great rejuvenation of the Chinese nation. New problems and new contradictions show that the path is filled with difficulties. the protection of the rule of law is urgently needed to carry out the great struggle, build the great project, boost the great cause. In the report of the 19th National Congress of the Communist Party of China, Xi (2017a, b) clearly put forward that as socialism with Chinese characteristics has entered a new era, the principal contradiction facing Chinese society has evolved into the contradiction between unbalanced and inadequate development and the people's ever-growing needs for a better life. This important judgment not only points out a new development direction for the construction of economy, politics, culture, society, and ecological civilization in the new era, but also provides decision-making basis and theoretical support for realizing the great dream. The realization of the Chinese dream of the great rejuvenation of the Chinese nation has entered a critical stage. On the path of rejuvenation, the Party and the country are also faced with multiple tasks, risks and challenges. In order to consolidate the ruling foundation of the path of rejuvenation and safeguard the basic rights of the people, it is increasingly expected that the Party and the country will further deepen the reform in the field of the rule of law by implementing the basic strategy of overall law-based governance, improve the rule of law system to promote common prosperity and social justice, with a view to effectively respond to the new needs of the people for the rule of law (Gong 2022).

To comprehensively promote the path of Chinese rule of law modernization and build a socialist rule of law system and country under the rule of law is not only the important content and internal goal of realizing the great rejuvenation of the Chinese nation, but also the institutional impetus and action guarantee of the rejuvenation of the Chinese nation. Strengthening the rule of law is a prerequisite for reinvigorating the nation and state. At present, China is in a critical period for achieving the rejuvenation of the Chinese nation, the evolution of the world's profound changes of a kind unseen in a century is accelerating, promoting reform, development and stability remains an arduous and heavy task, and opening up is deepening. We shall give a better play to the role of the rule of law in consolidating the foundations, keeping expectations stable, and serve long-term purposes (Xi 2022). To realize the great rejuvenation of the Chinese nation, we shall put the advancement of law-based governance across all fields of endeavor in a more prominent and important overall, fundamental and strategic position.

3. "Four Greatness" and the Basic Principles of the Path of Chinese Rule of Law Modernization

The realization of the overall objectives of the path of Chinese rule of law modernization must always adhere to the organic unity of the leadership of the CPC, the people running the country, and law-based governance of the country; integrate the rule of law and the rule by virtue and ensure that the rule of law and the rule by virtue complement each other; and insist on starting from the Chinese conditions.

First, Chinese rule of law modernization shall uphold the Party's leadership. The leadership of the CPC is the choice of history and the people. This leadership is vital for the future of the country, the nation, and the Party itself. Party leadership is the most essential attribute of socialism with Chinese characteristics, the greatest strength of the socialist system with Chinese characteristics, and the most fundamental guarantee of socialist rule of law. The leadership of the CPC shall underpin the path to modernization of the rule of law with Chinese characteristics throughout the process and in all aspects. To adhere to the leadership of the Party is to carry out the leadership of the Party throughout the whole process and all aspects of the path of Chinese rule of law modernization. The Party provides guidance for legislation, guarantees law enforcement, supports judicial justice, and plays an exemplary role in abiding by the law.

Second, in the modernization of the Chinese rule of law, the principle of people orientation shall be insisted on. That the people run the country is the essence and core requirement of socialist rule of law. The establishment of the socialist market economic system has built a broad social and economic soil for the elaboration of people-oriented concepts such as respecting people and showing concern to people's well-being. In this context, the CPC Central Committee put forward the strategic concept of committing to a people-centered approach and "people's well-being shall be concerned for"; The Fourth Plenary Session of the 18th CPC Central Committee took "people-oriented" as the core concept and goal of the construction of the rule of law; it was stressed in the central conference on the work of overall law-based governance that the overall law-based country governance must always "commit to a people-centered approach".

Third, Chinese rule of law modernization must adhere to the principle of equality before the law. Equality is the basic attribute of socialist law. The principle of equality before the law emphasizes that citizens and organizations are in an equal position in enjoying rights and assuming obligations, and no one is allowed to have privileges beyond the law. To uphold equality before the law, we must ensure that all citizens and organizations enjoy the rights and perform the obligations stipulated in the Constitution and the law equally; At the same time, the legitimate rights and interests of citizens and organizations are equally protected, and illegal acts are investigated according to law; Before the law, no citizen or organization is allowed to enjoy privileges beyond the law. Chinese rule of law modernization shall adhere to equality before the law and safeguard social fairness and justice.

Fourth, Chinese rule of law modernization requires the combination of rule of law and rule of virtue. National and social governance requires the joint role of law and morality. Morality is the foundation of the rule of law, and the rule of law is the guarantee of morality. Xi (2014) once stressed that law is written morality, while morality is conscious law. To adhere to the integration of rule of law and rule of virtue, we need to lay emphasis on both the rule of law and the rule of virtue, ensuring both the role of the law in regulating behaviors and the role of ethics in shaping the mind, so that law and virtue promote and enhance each other and rule of law and rule of virtue complement each other; to adhere to the integration of rule of law and rule of virtue, we need to adhere to the unity of socialist rule of law and the promotion of socialist morality, build a socialist culture of rule of law, carry out in-depth publicity and education of the rule of law and ideological and moral education, guide the whole people to establish a sense of rule of law, create a social atmosphere of law-abiding for the whole people, promote multi-level and multi-disciplinary rule of law, and promote socialist core values.

Fifth, Chinese rule of law modernization must proceed from China's national conditions. The path, theoretical system and system of socialism with Chinese characteristics are basic national conditions of China and the fundamental principles of Chinese path of modernization of the rule of law in China. Proceeding from China's national conditions, it is necessary to summarize and apply the successful experience of the Party in leading the people to implement the rule of law, focus on major theoretical and practical issues of socialist rule of law construction, draw on the essence of Chinese legal culture, learn from the beneficial experience of foreign rule of law, develop a socialist rule of law theory with Chinese characteristics that conforms to China's reality, reflects the law of social development, and provides theoretical guidance and support for the Chinese rule of law path.

4.3 Chinese Rule of Law Modernization and Modernization of National Governance Capacity and System

1. Strategic Arrangement for Modernization of National Governance Capacity and System

Adhering to and improving the socialist system with Chinese characteristics and promoting the modernization of the country's governance system and capacity is a major strategic decision to realize the great rejuvenation of the Chinese nation. The modernization of the national governance system and capacity is to make the national governance system institutionalized, scientific, standardized and procedural, so as to transform the institutional advantages of various aspects of socialism with Chinese characteristics into the effectiveness of governance.

Generally speaking, the basic elements of the modernization of the governance capacity of the national governance system include the following aspects: first, institutionalization. Institutional construction is the basic project for the modernization of the governance system of national governance capacity. The socialist system with Chinese characteristics is a scientific system formed by the Party and the people in the long-term practice and exploration. All work and activities of China's national governance are carried out in accordance with the socialist system with Chinese characteristics. China's national governance system and governance capacity are the concentrated embodiment of the socialist system with Chinese characteristics and its implementation capacity (Xia 2019). Second, participation or democratization. The modern national governance system is a democratic governance system, and the generation and operation of its public power must follow democratic rules, so that all sectors of society and the public have the institutional arrangement and space to participate in national governance and social governance. National governance can insist on taking the people as the center and ensure that the people are the masters of the country. Third, multiple governance. The national governance system is not a simple adjustment mode, but needs the joint promotion of various governance modes and methods such as politics, law, morality, religion, culture, etc. Among various adjustment modes, legal governance as the main line has basic and protective functions. Fourth, supervision. The supervision system of national governance and social governance can effectively prevent all kinds of nonstandard and illegal behaviors, ensure the institutionalization and standardization of the operation of public power, and maintain a series of systems and procedures for the operation of social power and public order. Fifth, efficiency. A modern national governance system should be scientific, strategic, systematic and effective, which is conducive to improving administrative efficiency and economic efficiency and effectively maintaining social stability and order. Sixth, the rule of law. The rule of law is an important support and guarantee for the national governance system and capacity. The basic way of national governance and social governance is the rule of law. The modernization of national governance and social governance depends on the rule of law in all fields. It is essential to utilize the advantages of the rule of law, such as predictability, operability, and accessibility, to consolidate social consensus during the transitional period. This will enable different stakeholders to pursue and achieve their maximum interests within the framework of the law and promote the modernization of the national governance system and governance capacity in accordance with the rule of law.

2. Promotion of Modernization of National Governance Capacity and Governance System

To realize the great rejuvenation of the Chinese nation, we need to focus on promoting the modernization of the governance capacity of the national governance system, and comprehensively improve and develop the socialist system with Chinese characteristics. To promote the modernization of the governance capacity of the national governance system, we need to comprehensively promote the rule of law. The rule of law is the basic way to regulate social interests, the concentrated embodiment of social fairness and justice, and the most important foundation for the construction of socialist system with Chinese characteristics.

First of all, the rule of law is the inherent need for modernization of the governance capacity of the national governance system. It is well known that the basic socio-economic condition for national governance and social governance is the socialist market economy, which requires the market mechanism to scientifically and reasonably allocate resources. The operation and development of the socialist market economy is always inseparable from the rule of law. In a sense, the market economy is essentially a rule of law economy. Secondly, promoting the modernization of the governance capacity of the national governance system is a systematic project, which cannot be separated from the path of the rule of law. In the process of modernization of the governance capacity of the national governance system, in fact, we need to face various social contradictions and conflicts, and we need multifaceted and multi-level reform measures. China's reform is sailing in uncharted waters with tough challenges., and the international situation is complex and volatile. Our Party is faced with an unprecedented task of reform, development and stability, an unprecedented number of contradictions, risks and challenges, and the rule of law plays a more prominent and important role in the overall work of the Party and the country (The CPC Central Committee 2014: 2). In addition, promoting the legalization of national governance is not only a beneficial guarantee and goal of developing socialism with Chinese characteristics, but also a major measure to modernize the governance capacity of the national governance system. Realizing the modernization of national governance is bound to require the full involvement of the rule of law. Chinese rule of law path is an important way to realize the modernization of national governance. To promote the modernization of the governance capacity of the national governance system is to promote and realize the legalization, democratization, scientization and informatization of the national governance system and governance capacity, and its focus is to promote the legalization of national governance.

3. Improvement of the Party's Capacity for and Performance in Governance

The modernization of the governance capability of the national governance system includes not only the narrow sense of national governance, but also the Party's governance capability and leadership level. The modernization of the governance capacity of the national governance system cannot be separated from the improvement of the Party's governance ability and level.

The governance capacity of the Party is the ability of the Party to lead the state power, economic and cultural undertakings and social affairs, which is carried out through the ruling system, ways and means. The fourth plenary session of the 16th

CPC Central Committee put forward the concept of scientific governance, democratic governance, and law-based governance. Scientific governance emphasizes that governance should conform to the law, and use scientific ideas, systems and methods to allocate and use power and govern the country; Democratic governance means that the Party should adhere to governing for the people, ensure that the people are the masters of the country, and utilize power and manage the country through democratic systems and procedures; Ruling by law is the guarantee of the Party's governance capacity. Under the background of Chinese path to modernization of the rule of law, improving the Party's governance capacity needs to be carried out through ruling by law. Ruling by law is the institutional requirement of building socialism with Chinese characteristics and the practical requirement of realizing the great rejuvenation of the Chinese nation. Ruling by law needs to adapt to the rule of law trend of social and economic development, actively use legal means to control social development, adjust various interests, and be good at solving various contradictions and problems within the framework of the rule of law. By exercising power according to law, we will implement the Party's will, line, principles and policies in all aspects of economic, political, cultural, social and ecological civilization construction, and improve the Party's ability to cope with the governance test and resist risks. Maintaining the authority of the Constitution and the law is the basic requirement of ruling by law. The ruling behavior of the Party should conform to the spirit of the rule of law, the principles of the rule of law and the legal norms and use the Constitution and laws to govern the country and society. To this end, to govern according to law, the first is to improve the Party's ability to lead legislation, ensure law enforcement, support justice, and take the lead in abiding by the law.

4.4 Chinese Rule of Law Modernization and Construction of Socialist Rule of Law System

1. Building a Socialist Rule of Law System with Chinese Characteristics

Building a socialist legal system with Chinese characteristics means, under the leadership of the CPC, adhering to the socialist system with Chinese characteristics, implementing the socialist theory of the rule of law with Chinese characteristics, forming a complete system of legal norms, an efficient system of rule of law implementation, a strict system of rule of law supervision, a strong system of rule of law guarantee, and establishing a sound system of intra-Party laws and regulations (The CPC Central Committee 2014: 4). In the overall goal of Chinese path to the modernization of the rule of law with Chinese characteristics, the construction of the socialist rule of law system with Chinese characteristics has a fundamental position.

The socialist system of rule of law with Chinese characteristics is the key to promoting the comprehensive rule of law. We should adhere to the integration of rule of law and rule of virtue and realize that the rule of law and rule of virtue complement each other. We should actively promote legislation in such important areas as national security, scientific and technological innovation, public health, bio-safety, ecological civilization, risk prevention, and foreign-related rule of law, improve the legal system urgently needed for national governance, and the legal system necessary to meet the growing needs of the people for a better life, and ensure the healthy development of new business forms and new models with good law and good governance (Xi 2021).

2. Building a Comprehensive Legal System and an Efficient Legal Implementation System

To build a comprehensive legal system of legal norms, we must adhere to the concept of putting people first and legislation for the people, implement the core socialist values, and make every legislation conform to the spirit of the Constitution, reflect the will of the people, and be supported by the people. We shall put the principles of justice, fairness and openness through the whole process of legislation, improve the legislative system and mechanism, adhere to the simultaneous development of legislation, reform, abolishment and interpretation, and enhance the timeliness, systematism, pertinence and effectiveness of laws and regulations (The CPC Central Committee 2014: 8). To this end, for one thing, we should speed up the legislation in key areas, and at the same time as all national undertakings and work are brought into the track of the rule of law (Xi 2022). For another, it is necessary to improve the legislative procedures of the legal regulatory system. The key is to address prominent issues such as the lack of coordination and consistency among legal departments and regulations in the existing legal framework, as well as inadequate systematization. Efforts should be made to address the problem of missing laws and regulations in the existing legal framework, especially to adapt to the changes in socio-economic development and enhance the systematic nature of laws and regulations. Moreover, attention should be given to enhancing the scientific level of some laws and regulations and improving their operability and applicability.

3. Building a Stringent Scrutiny System and an Effective Guarantee System

To advance law-based governance, we shall build a stringent scrutiny system. Through internal Party scrutiny, scrutiny by people's congresses, scrutiny by other political parties, administrative scrutiny, judicial scrutiny, scrutiny through auditing, public scrutiny, and scrutiny by the media, we can restrict and standardize public power, safeguard and safeguard civil rights, and make the rule of law truly implemented.

Strict law enforcement and fair justice are inseparable from strong supervision of the implementation of the law. Only by strengthening the supervision of the implementation of the law can we prevent and correct the tendency of replacing the law with words, abusing the law by relying on power, and bending the law for selfish ends, prevent and correct the tendency of disobedience to the law and lax enforcement of the law, and form the trend of abiding by the law in the whole society, and the socialist rule of law will have authority and vitality.

The guarantee system generally includes political guarantee, ideological guarantee, organizational guarantee and operational guarantee. Adhering to the Party's leadership is the political guarantee of socialist rule of law; The ideological guarantee of the socialist rule of law is to implement the theory of rule of law with Chinese characteristics and strengthen the awareness of the members of society; The construction of the legal work force is the organization and talent guarantee in the socialist legal guarantee system; The establishment and effective implementation of a scientific index system and assessment criteria for the construction of the rule of law is the operational guarantee of the socialist rule of law (Zhang 2014).

A strong guarantee system for the rule of law is an inevitable requirement to promote the construction of China under the rule of law, an important measure to promote social fairness and justice, and the well-being of the people, and an important means to implement the Constitution and laws. Only if the security system is scientific, the mechanism is sound, and the resources are sufficient, can we ensure strict law enforcement, fair justice, and provide the basis for the unified and correct implementation of the Constitution and laws.

4. Building a Sound System of Party Rules and Regulations

A sound system of Party rules and regulations is not only the need to adapt to Chinese path to the modernization of the rule of law, but also the internal requirement to strengthen the Party's construction and further enhance the Party's governing capacity. As the governing party, strengthening the standardization and systematization of laws and regulations within the party, and adhering to the principle of governing by science, democracy and law within the scope of the Constitution are important ways and means to promote party building, maintain the progressiveness and vitality of the party. A sound Party legal system should be coordinated with the national legal system, which is a mutually supporting and benign interaction relationship. The construction of Party rules and regulations needs to adhere to the changes in the times and the strategic guidelines of the Party. It is necessary to make timely adjustments, revisions, and clearances to existing norms, regulations, and other standards in order to build and form a comprehensive and effective system of Party rules and regulations. This will ensure the comprehensive and effective implementation of the tasks of law-based governance, law-based exercise of state power.

4.5 Basically Building a Country, Government, and Society Based on the Rule of Law

1. Goal Orientation

The 19th National Congress of the Communist Party of China put forward the "two stages" strategy for the construction of China under the rule of law in the future. In the first stage from 2020 to 2035, we will build on the foundation created by the moderately prosperous society with a further 15 years of hard work to see that socialist modernization is basically realized. The vision is that by the end of this stage, the rule of law for the country, the government, and society is basically in place. In the second stage from 2035 to the middle of the twenty-first century, we will, building on having basically achieved modernization, work hard for a further 15 years and develop China into a great modern socialist country that is prosperous, strong, democratic, culturally advanced, harmonious, and beautiful. By the end of this stage, the following goals will have been met: new heights are reached in every dimension of material, political, cultural and ethical, social, and ecological advancement. Modernization of China's system and capacity for governance is achieved (Xi 2017a, b). It is the most visible and representative objective in basically realizing the modernization of the country under the rule of law that the rule of law for the country, the government, and society is basically in place.

The process of the path of Chinese rule of law modernization is a profound rule of law revolution. In the process of the rule of law revolution, rule of law for the country, the government, and society are interconnected, forming the organic whole of the rule of law China (Gong 2018). A country ruled by law is the goal of the building of a government and society ruled by law. The building of a government and society ruled by law must obey and serve the building of a country ruled by law; A government ruled by law is the main body and focus of the building of a country ruled by law, and play a leading and exemplary role in the building of a society ruled by law; A society ruled by law is the foundation and support of the building of a country and a government ruled by law. The building of a country and a government ruled by law must build a solid foundation of rule of law for the society (Yuan 2020).

2. Strategic Layout

Firstly, we shall adhere to comprehensively promoting sound legislation, strict law enforcement, impartial administration of justice, and the observance of law by everyone. Scientific legislation means that every legislation conforms to the spirit of the Constitution, reflects the will of the people and is supported by the people. Scientific legislation needs to improve the socialist legal system with Chinese characteristics with the Constitution as the core, and reflect the status of the Constitution as the fundamental law in the legal system; Scientific legislation needs to clarify the focus of legislation in the new era, especially with the basic guidance of protecting property rights, maintaining contracts, unifying the market, equal exchange, fair competition, and effective supervision, to carry out legislation on the protection of the rights and interests of the main body of the socialist market economy, the stability of market order, and the guarantee of economic development; Scientific legislation needs to strengthen the concept of the rule of law of the legislative staff, especially the cultivation of the concept of "people-oriented" and "legislation for the people".

Strict law enforcement means that governments at all levels must adhere to the leadership of the Party and on the track of the rule of law to innovate the law enforcement system, improve the law enforcement procedures, promote comprehensive law enforcement, strictly enforce the law enforcement responsibilities, establish a unified, authoritative and efficient administrative system according to law, and accelerate the construction of a government under the rule of law with scientific functions, legal powers and responsibilities, strict law enforcement, openness and fairness, integrity and efficiency, and law-abiding integrity (The CPC Central Committee 2014: 15).

Strict law enforcement requires the establishment and improvement of a law-based decision-making mechanism, the full performance of government functions in accordance with the law, and the establishment of a lifelong accountability system for major decisions and an responsibility retracing mechanism; We need to deepen the reform of the administrative law enforcement system, improve the legal system of administrative organizations and administrative procedures, promote the legalization of institutions, functions, authorities, procedures and responsibilities, see that law is enforced in a strict, standardized, fair, and civil way, and adhere to the principles that statutory duties must be fulfilled, and no action may be taken without legal authority; We need to strengthen the power restraints and supervision of the contingent of personnel for administrative enforcement of laws, establish a mechanism for administrative agencies to review the legality of their major decisions, work to codify its structure, functions, powers, procedures, and responsibilities into law; and exercise powers that are clearly defined, and advance the regulation and lawfulness of powers of the governments at all levels (Xi 2017a, b).

Impartial administration of justice means that the judicial administration system and the judicial power operation mechanism shall be improved, judicial actions shall be regulated, supervision over judicial activities shall be strengthened, and efforts shall be made to ensure that people percept fairness and justice in each judicial case. Impartial administration of justice needs to improve systems for ensuring the law-based, independent, and impartial exercise of judicial and procuratorial powers. The authority at all levels within judicial organs shall be defined, with perfection of mechanisms for internal supervision and inhibition; The fair administration of justice needs to deepen reform of the judicial law system; optimize the allocation of judicial functions; standardize judicial activities; and create a socialist judicial system that is fair, effective and authoritative; Impartial administration of justice needs to improve the legal system that that facts are used as basis and the law as the criterion, cases shall be handled in strict accordance with facts and the law, the case-handling process conforms to procedural justice, and case-handling results conforms to substantial justice (The CPC Central Committee 2014: 15). Impartial administration of justice needs to ensure the participation of the masses of the people in the administration of justice, strengthen the judicial protection of human rights, and enable people to access to fairness and justice. We must promote judicial impartiality and credibility through greater openness, establish a judiciary system that is open, dynamic, transparent, and accessible to the public, put an end to backroom dealings, and resolutely fight judicial corruption (Xi 2017a, b: 131).

The law-abiding of the whole people means we must promote the socialist rule of law, develop a socialist rule of law culture, encourage all members of society to show greater enthusiasm for and initiative in promoting the rule of law, and create an atmosphere in which people feel it is honorable to abide by the law while disgraceful to break the law, so that all our people will faithfully advocate, consciously observe, and firmly safeguard the socialist rule of law (The CPC Central Committee 2014: 26). The socialist consciousness of rule of law embodies the spirit of rule of law, which is the organic unity of the Party's leadership, the people's ownership of the country and the rule of law. The comprehensive promotion of the rule of law cannot be separated from the cultivation of socialist awareness of the rule of law. We will continue to take the popularization and observance of the law by the whole people as the long-term basic work of governing the country according to law, carry out in-depth publicity and education on the rule of law, and guide the whole people to consciously abide by the law, find the law in case of trouble, and rely on the law to solve problems.

Secondly, we shall adhere to parallel progress in the rule of law for national governance, exercise of state power, and government administration. At the Central Conference on the Work of Comprehensive Law-based Country Governance, *Xi Jinping* stressed that we must push forward coordinated progress in law-based governance, exercise of state power, and government administration, and promote the integrated development of the law-based country, government, and society. Comprehensive law-based of law is a systemic project; we need to plan it in an integrated way, with greater emphasis on a systemic, holistic and coordinated approach (Xi 2021). Law-based governance, law-based exercise of state power, and law-based administration of government are closely connected and mutually supportive.

Law-based governance is in terms of national and social governance, law-based exercise of state power is in terms of the Party's construction and governance mode, and law-based administration of government is the requirement of the government's own construction. "coordinated progress" conforms to the law of the modernization of the Chinese rule of law. Any country and social affairs are interrelated and cannot be viewed separately. To practice the rule of law in a country requires law-based governance and the building of a country ruled by law and society ruled by law; The leadership of the Party insists on the rule of law, which requires law-based exercise of state power; The government's pursuit of the rule of law requires law-based administration of government and the building of a government ruled by law (Ma 2019).

Thirdly, we shall adhere to the integrated building of a country ruled by law, government ruled by law and society ruled by law. At the 19th National Congress of the Communist Party of China, it has been set as an important objective of basically realizing socialist modernization by 2035 that the rule of law for the country, the government, and society will be basically in place, and has started a new journey of comprehensive law-based governance in a new era. To basically build a country ruled by law, a government ruled by law and a society ruled by law, we need to adhere to coordinated progress in law-based governance, law-based exercise of state power, and law-based administration of government and integrated building of the rule of law for the country, the government, and society. In the first stage of China's rule of law modernization process in the new era from 2020 to 2035, the rule of law for the country, the government, and society will be basically in place, which profoundly reflects the direction of Chinese rule of law modernization in the new era, and undoubtedly marks rule of law in China in place (Gong 2018).

As three pillars of the building of the rule of law, the rule of law for the country, the government, and society are mutually connected and internally united. In the process of basically building the rule of law for the country, the government, and society, we must promote synchronous plan, simultaneous implementation, and integrated building of the rule of law for the country, the government, and society.

Adhering to the "integrated building" is the internal requirement of coordinating and promoting the strategic layout of "four comprehensives". Coordinated promotion of the strategic layout of "four comprehensives" is the major strategy of governance established by the Party Central Committee with Comrade *Xi Jinping* as the core. Law-based governance is not only an important part of the strategic layout of "four comprehensives", but also an important guarantee of the strategic layout of "four comprehensives". Adhering to the "integrated building" can better meet the people's growing demands for democracy, the rule of law, fairness and justice. Only by adhering to the "integrated building" can the people really feel fairness and justice, and have more sense of happiness and security.

Adhering to "integrated building" is also an inevitable requirement for comprehensively deepening reform. The unity of advancing reforms under the rule of law and improving the rule of law in reforms shall be adhered to. Only by adhering to integrated building and promoting reform with the rule of law thinking and way can we better play the role of the rule of law in guiding, standardizing and ensuring reform, confirm and consolidate the results of reform in a timely manner, and ensure that reform in all fields and in all aspects is always comprehensively promoted on the track of the rule of law. Chinese path to the modernization of the rule of law is a huge systematic project, which must be comprehensively considered and planned. Adhering to the integrated building can bring together all forces, achieve the complete and effective operation of the system at all levels of the country, government and society, and vigorously promote the building of a socialist country under the rule of law in China.

The rule of law for the country, the government and society complement each other. The rule of law for the country is the goal, the rule of law for the government is the subject, and the rule of law for the society is the foundation. A country ruled by law is the goal of the building of a government ruled by law and a society ruled by law. The building of a government ruled by law and a society ruled by law should closely focus on the goal of building a socialist country ruled by law, innovate the system, improve the system and mechanism, and clarify the work tasks. A government ruled by law is the focus of the building of a country ruled by law. "integrated building" should not only adhere to the systematic promotion, but also adhere to the key development, and strengthen the building of a government ruled by law.

3. Human Resources

The building of the team of the work on the rule of law is the organization and talent guarantee of the new path of the modernization of the Chinese rule of law. To comprehensively advance the law-based governance of the country, we must channel great energy into raising the levels of political integrity and professional competence and ethics of the rule of law professionals and strive to develop a contingent of professionals devoted to the socialist rule of law and loyal to the Party, the country, the people, and the law (The CPC Central Committee 2014: 30). Raising the level of competence of rule of law professionals is the need of all tasks of the modernization of

Chinese rule of law. To implement the basic strategy of comprehensively advancing the law-based governance of the country, adhere to the common promotion of law-based governance, law-based exercise of state power, and law-based administration of government, and adhere to the integrated building of the rule of law for the country, the government, and society, we cannot do without a high-quality legal work team.

To build a contingent of highly competent rule of law professionals, we need to give top priority to strengthening their political integrity. the education of core socialist values and the socialist idea of the rule of law shall be conducted in depth, professional ethics and morality shall be strengthened, and efforts shall be made to establish political and legal affairs team with firm faith, enforcing the law for the people, brave to assume responsibility, and of integrity and cleanness, strive to develop a contingent of professionals devoted to the socialist rule of law and loyal to the Party, the country, the people, and the law. Secondly, we should increase the levels of standardization, specialization, and professionalism among rule of law professionals; improve the system for certifying legal professionals; establish a system for recruiting eligible lawyers and legal experts into the ranks of legislators, judges, and public procurators; build a more standardized and convenient mechanism for recruiting university graduates majoring in law; and improve the system of job security for rule of law professionals. Third, we need to raise the level of competence of legal service providers, prompt lawyers to become more self-motivated and resolute in following the path of socialist rule of law with Chinese characteristics, and build a well-mixed contingent of private, government, and corporate lawyers who complement each other's strengths.

The path of Chinese rule of law modernization provides guidance for the construction of the rule of law workforce, as well as presents new requirements for legal education and the cultivation of rule of law talents. The innovation of the rule of law talent cultivation mechanism and the cultivation of high-quality legal professionals are not only the fundamental goals and tasks of the construction of the rule of law workforce but also the foundation of the path of Chinese rule of law modernization. We should implement the socialist rule of law thought with Chinese characteristics in the new era in the preparation of teaching materials and teaching work in the law disciplines, ensure that this thought is incorporated into the curriculum and made a way of thinking, and strive to cultivate more rule of law talents with strong ideals and beliefs, ardent feelings of patriotism, and solid jurisprudential roots. We should promote universal compliance with the law as a basic project and fully carry out a responsibility program in which state law enforcement departments are responsible for strengthening public legal awareness. All officials should take the lead in respecting, learning, abiding by and using the law, and guide the public in consciously abiding by the law, using the law to resolve cases, and solving problems with the law. We should review the experience of the building and practice of Chinese rule of law system, communicate of the best of Chinese traditional rule of law culture, tell the story of Chinese rule of law well, and ensure Chinese rule of law system and theory have greater influence and a bigger say internationally (Xi 2022).

4.6 Conclusion

Since the 18th CPC National Congress, the Party Central Committee with Comrade *Xi jinping* as its core has incorporated the comprehensive rule of law into the Chinese dream of realizing the great rejuvenation of the Chinese nation from the strategic perspective of the future and destiny of the Party and the country, embarking on a grand, comprehensive and magnificent path of Chinese rule of law modernization. The realization of the great rejuvenation of the Chinese nation is inseparable from the realization of the overall objectives of the path of Chinese rule of law modernization. The promotion of the path of Chinese rule of law modernization should not only achieve the overall goal of building a socialist rule of law system with Chinese characteristics and building a socialist country ruled by law, which is to be achieved by the comprehensive rule of law. Moreover, as the main component of the modernization of the governance capacity of the national governance system, the modernization of the governance capacity of the national governance system is regarded as the major goal of path to the rule of law, so that the modernization of the governance system of the national governance capacity can be fully promoted on the track of the rule of law.

References

China Institute of CPC Literature Research. 2014. D*ecision of the central committee of the communist party of China on several major issues concerning comprehensively promoting the rule of law.* People's Publishing House.

Gong, P. 2018. The strategic arrangement of China's rule of law modernization in the new era. *China Legal Science*, 3, 27–50. https://doi.org/10.14111/j.cnki.zgfx.2018.03.002

Gong, P. 2022. Common prosperity and social justice: important features of the new path to modernization of Chinese rule of law. *Democracy and Legal System Weekly*, 1.

Ma, H. 2019. Pursue coordinated progress in law-based governance, exercise of state power and law-based government administration to promote the integrated development of rule of law for the country, the government, and society. *Legal Daily*.

Xi, J. 2014. *Xi Jinping: the governance of China I.* Foreign Language Press.

Xi, J. 2017a. *Xi Jinping: the governance of China II.* Foreign Language Press.

Xi, J. 2017b. Secure a decisive victory in building a moderately prosperous society in all respects and strive for the great success of socialism with Chinese characteristics for a new era. *People's Daily*.

Xi, J. 2021. Firmly taking the socialist rule of law path with Chinese characteristics in the new era to provide support for building a modern socialist country in all respects. *Qiushi* 5: 4–6.

Xi, J. 2022. Adhere to the path of socialist rule of law with Chinese characteristics and better promote the construction of socialist rule of law system with Chinese characteristics. *Qiushi*, 4.

Xia, J. 2019. China's exploration of modernization of national governance system and governance capacity. *Guangming Daily*.

Yuan, S. 2020. Adhering to the integrated construction of the country, government and society ruled by law. *People's Daily*.

Zhang, W. 2014. Vigorously strengthening the legal work force. *People's Court Daily*.

Chapter 5
Promotion Model of Chinese Rule of Law Path

Abstract The bottom-up social evolution model, the top-down government-driven model, and the combination of top-down and bottom-up models are three different types of approaches for advancing the modernization of the rule of law. The interaction between government-driven initiatives and social evolution, as well as the bidirectional interaction between top-down and bottom-up approaches, constitute the notable characteristics of the advancement of Chinese rule of law path.

5.1 Introduction

A comprehensive survey of the process of modernization of the rule of law in the world shows that the type of the modernization of the rule of law can be divided into two types: endogenous and exogenous. The former refers to the type of modernization of the rule of law that the initial driving force produces in the society, and the latter refers to the type of modernization of the rule of law that the initial driving force comes from the external impact or challenge of the society. However, special national characteristics of rule of law in China determine the unique nature of the way to promote the path of Chinese rule of law modernization. China is a socialist Eastern country with a large population, vast territory, diverse ethnicities, and a complex national situation. To achieve long-term governance in such a large country, the CPC must thoroughly analyze the economic, political, social, cultural, historical and even geographical conditions or factors that exist in the Chinese society in a changing state. In this way, there are thus innumerable interwoven forces, an infinite number of parallelograms of forces, productive of one result—the historical event which itself may be seen as the product of a power operating unconsciously and involuntarily as a whole (Marx and Engels 2009: 592).

In the historical resultant force formed by the interaction of "an infinite number of parallelograms of forces" in the process of modernization of Chinese rule of law, the internal interaction between government promotion and social evolution is the logical representation and realistic carrier of this "historical resultant force". President *Xi Jinping* attaches great importance to the study of the way to promote

© The Author(s), under exclusive license to Springer Nature Singapore Pte Ltd. 2024
X. Dong and J. Guo, *Chinese Rule of Law Path and Cultivation of Foreign-Related Rule of Law Talents*, https://doi.org/10.1007/978-981-97-2313-3_5

the path of Chinese rule of law modernization. On the basis of a profound summary of the basic laws of the modernization of the rule of law in the world, Xi (2020: 135–136) elaborated three different types of promoting the rule of law, pointing out that from the perspective of the development process of countries that have achieved modernization, western countries such as the United Kingdom, the United States, France and so on have presented a top-down social evolution model, that is, to adapt to the needs of market economy and modernization development, and gradually realize the rule of law after one or two hundred years or even two or three hundred years of evolution, and the government's role in promoting the rule of law is relatively small. For example, Singapore, South Korea, Japan and so on, the main presentation is the government from the top In the next few decades, the rule of law has been rapidly promoted, and the government has played a great role in promoting the rule of law. Taking the relationship between government promotion and social evolution as an analytical dimension, this important exposition not only insightfully reveals the main characteristics of the three different types of approaches in the process of global rule of law modernization, but also profoundly interprets the notable features of the approach to advancing the modernization of the rule of law with Chinese characteristics. It has made an important contribution to the development of Marxist legal theory and has provided guidance for an in-depth exploration of the morphological features and intrinsic mechanisms of the modernization of the rule of law with Chinese characteristics.

5.2 Bottom-Up Evolution Modernization Model of the Rule of Law

Generally speaking, the bottom-up evolution model of the modernization of the rule of law, or the social evolution of the modernization of the rule of law, mainly refers to the transformation and development process of the rule of law from the traditional rule of law to the modern rule of law due to the maturity of the social internal conditions. This type of bottom-up promotion of the modernization of the rule of law is generally represented by the United Kingdom, the United States, France and other European and American countries.

On the whole, the social evolution model of rule of law modernization has developed gradually due to the gradual maturity of social internal conditions. In the process of the formation of modern western legal system, the civil society revolution in the Middle Ages of Western Europe undoubtedly became the profound social and historical basis of modern rational law and created the main structure of modern law. During this period, although feudal customs, king's orders and even the customary rights of the aristocracy still played an important role in the social adjustment system, the positive function of the law has been clearly reflected. The emergence of the new commercial law system itself means that the large-scale commodity trading activities and the urgent demand of the civil class with the emerging merchant groups as the main body for the law. At the same time, it also shows the dynamic reflection and promotion of law to social and economic changes. Although the feudal lords still dominated the judicial process, the practice of making full-time judgments by legally trained officials has been taken seriously. The formation of the commercial court system shows the establishment of the legal autonomy of the merchant group. The urban organization system established according to the city charter is divided into legislative, administrative and judicial departments that have restrictive relations with each other. The unique status of the judiciary has been confirmed. In addition, the struggle of the early merchant class, the predecessor of the modern bourgeoisie, against the feudal legal system that was hostile to it, also had an important impact on the legal reform of modern Western European society. And so on. These factors or conditions gradually generated from within the society provide a deep social source of modern law (Michael 2000). From about the thirteenth century, with the promulgation of the Magna Carta (June 1215), Britain began to change to the modern rule of law. The direct source of American law is English law. The basic substratum of American law, as of American speech, is English (Lawrence 2019).

In Britain, the United States, France and other countries that first embarked on the path of capitalist modernization, the process of creating and forming the modern rule of law is a natural and gradual social process, although it is full of many major social change events. Admittedly, the influence of the government on the development of the rule of law cannot be ignored, but in general, the role of the government is relatively limited. However, it should be noted that the role of the state needs to be given sufficient attention in the formation of modern rational formalistic law in Western Europe. The country in this period was neither a typical feudal country nor a modern capitalist country, but an autocratic country. Western European autocratic countries are a special type of state form and a community of national interests. In the late Middle Ages, the nation-state was gradually established to meet the needs of society. By the beginning of the sixteenth century, the autocratic monarchical nation-state regime had almost become the universal regime in Western Europe. This autocratic monarchy and its nation-state are called the so-called rational state by thinkers. As Marx (1956: 128) said, thinkers from *Machiavelli* to *Hegel* have begun to observe the country from a human perspective. They derive the natural laws of the country from reason and experience rather than from theology. Among them, political ideas may be very different, but they seem to have a common orientation, that is, they advocate that the governance of the country shall be based on the law. It is this belief that makes the concept of state in this period closely linked with the elements of law, and then makes the autocratic nation-state have a new connotation and characteristics. Therefore, the Western European autocratic countries, which formed in the late Middle Ages and embodied the spirit of rational countries, had a strong interest in creating a modern rational legal system from the beginning, and the legal system construction became an important field of state activities during this period. According to the needs of social development, the rulers of Western European autocratic monarchy countries have formulated laws and decrees to promote the development of law and have a strong interest in the inheritance and revival of Roman law. Although Roman law is the law of the pre-capitalist period, it contains the general provisions of most legal relations in the capitalist period and is the legal basis of the modern rational formalism legal movement. Therefore, the revival of Roman law was a major reform movement in the social life of Western Europe in the middle and late Middle Ages. It reflected the historical process of the gradual establishment of capitalist economic relations and the gradual transformation of the legal system in early modern times from the legal perspective. The monarchy and autocratic state have played a significant role in the development of the rediscovery of Roman law movement since the twelfth century. This is because the revival of Roman law reflects the legal requirements of the emerging civil class, and the autocratic monarch needs the support and support of the civil class in the struggle with the feudal aristocracy. By promoting the development of Roman law, the autocratic monarch meets the legal requirements of the civil class. However, from a deeper perspective, the autocratic monarch's emphasis on the creation of law and the development of Roman law actually reflects the needs of the monarch's own interests, and also reflects the basic requirements of the emerging economic relations on the national superstructure. In the struggle between kingship and religious power at the end of the Middle Ages, in order to realize the autocracy of monarchy, defeat the religious power, and defeat the lord, the kingship must reflect the economic needs of the emerging modern civil class, namely the bourgeoisie, and develop industry and commerce, so as to form an alliance against the church and the feudal hierarchy with the emerging civil class. At the same time, the kings in the late Middle Ages formulated many policies and laws to support businessmen and encourage them to carry out overseas trade and open up overseas markets. At the same time, *the Commercial Code* and *the Maritime Code*, which actively promote commercial development and foreign trade, have also been formulated and implemented. The development of industrial and commercial capitalism needs laws that can be as reliable as machines. The typical feature of this type of law is formalism. In the historical evolution of western law, *Roman law* is a law with formal rationality, which can be used by modern autocratic countries to create rational laws. The officials trained in *Roman law* are often administrative experts superior to all other officials. It was in this process that a rational formal modern legal system gradually grew and developed. From this point of view, Max (2012: 588) pointed out that from the standpoint of economic history, this fact is significant in that the alliance between the state and formal jurisprudence was indirectly favorable to capitalism. Therefore, the establishment of modern rational law in the West is inseparable from the promotion of autocratic countries.

It should be further pointed out that although many social factors and conditions gradually developed from within the western society have laid a social foundation for the western legal modernization movement, modern western law was not formed and developed in a completely closed environment and was also stimulated or challenged by many external factors, thus triggering a further reform process. In the growth of modern western legal civilization, the most decisive event was the discovery of the American continent in 1492. The great geographical discovery has strongly promoted the overseas trade expansion of Europe, which is crucial to the development of Europe itself. The great geographical discovery broke the closed state of the legal development in the Middle Ages of Western Europe, stimulated the colonial expansion of Europeans overseas and the desire to improve their inherent legal system, and showed the historical possibility of a new social order to Western European society, thus announcing the arrival of the modern era. In this regard, Marx (1960: 396) analyzed that the scope of activities that influence each other is increasingly expanding in the process of development, and the primitive state of isolation of all ethnic groups is more and more complete due to the increasingly perfect production mode, communication and the division of labor among all ethnic groups that have spontaneously developed, and history is becoming the history of the world to a greater extent. With the intensification of overseas expansion, industry and commerce have achieved rapid development. Commercial competition between countries is often carried out through wars or various prohibitions to protect tariffs, thus promoting the formation and development of new international relations and norms of international law.

5.3 Top-Down Evolution Modernization Model of the Rule of Law

The government-driven modernization of the rule of law, also known as the top-down modernization of the rule of law, mainly refers to the top-down growth and progress of the rule of law caused by the impact of foreign legal culture and the strong impetus of the government. This type is usually represented by Japan, Russia, South Korea, Singapore and other countries. In this type of modernization of the rule of law, government reform often becomes the historical precursor of the modernization of the rule of law, and the government plays a major role in promoting it. In countries and societies with this type of rule of law modernization, the original commodity economic factors are relatively weak and cannot spontaneously form the main force to change society. The government and modern political parties, as organized social forces, play a leading role in the process of rule of law modernization.

According to the analysis of modernization theory, as the main driving force of the government-driven modernization model of rule of law, the extent to which the government plays its role often depends on the behavior of the leading group in the government. The motivation and value belief of the reform are the important driving force system of leading group actions. In other words, why should the leading group, as the backbone of the government, aspire to promote social and legal reform and realize the modernization of the rule of law. In Japan, the leaders of the Meiji era came to power at the call of the restoration of imperial power. They were committed to restoring the functions of the Mikado. They achieved this goal by reminding people that the Mikado is a symbol of national unity, by moving the court from Kyoto to Tokyo, by rationalizing the new capital, and by unifying the functions of religious rituals and administrative management. However, although they publicly announced "enlightened monarchy" (Meiji), but the monarch did not rule. In his name, it is to make the bold actions of his government have legitimacy. If it is not in his name, those actions will have no legitimacy. The Constitution is a gift he gave to his people in vain. This view originates from the tradition, which puts the overall interests of the society above the local interests and personal interests. Under the driving force of this traditional consciousness, the ruling group in Japan greatly accelerated the country's process of modernization. Based on this system of values, they established a strong authority and a unified administrative system, as well as a unified legal code and judiciary system, thereby creating a new order and promoting the process of rule of law modernization. However, due to their devotion to the emperor as their duty and their attempt to use imperial power as a tool for reform and modernization, they paid little attention to radical restructuring of the social structure. This provided the social conditions for the rise of militarism and hindered the process of rule of law modernization in Japan.

It should be noted that in the government-driven model of rule of law modernization, there are various ways in which the state and government take action, broadly categorized into three main approaches. Firstly, establishing a strong bureaucratic system and state machinery to promote social transformation and legal transition. Secondly, establishing legal institutions and compiling written legal codes according to the goals of reform. Thirdly, mobilizing and organizing social resources to participate in the process of legal change. In the government-driven model of rule of law modernization, a significant task for the government and its leadership is to effectively mobilize and organize various classes or strata of society to participate in the process of legal reform. Intellectuals, military personnel, and farmers play important roles in this process. Compared to the societal evolution model of rule of law modernization, the role of the state and government is more prominent in the legal transformation and reform. Having a strong government system is a necessary condition for rapidly achieving social and legal reform in previously underdeveloped countries, and the extent to which the government's role is exercised often depends on the values, beliefs, and actions of the dominant leadership group within the government.

5.4 Modernization Model of the Rule of Law with Two-Way Interaction Between Bottom-Up and Top-Down

On the whole, the modernization model of the rule of law which is interactive from top to bottom and from bottom to top is also known as the modernization model of the rule of law driven by interaction between government promotion and social evolution. It usually means that under the interaction of various internal and external factors, the government and society form a pattern of interaction from top to bottom and from bottom to top, thus promoting the transforming and changing process from traditional legal system to modern rule of law system. This model is typical of China. The modernization model of the rule of law driven by interaction between government promotion and social evolution has both some characteristics of the modernization model of the rule of law driven by social evolution and the relevant attributes of the model of rule of law modernization driven by government promotion. The internal integration of the two forms a unique mixed type of modernization of the rule of law.

On the one hand, from the perspective of the generation mechanism of the modernization of the rule of law, the factors and foundations of the rule of law reform have gradually been generated within the country and society, thus providing important conditions for the formation and development of the rule of law reform movement. The historical process of China's legal system reform and modernization has its inherent special track, which is the result of a series of complex factors. Admittedly, the impact and influence of modern western legal culture on the legal system reform in modern China is undoubtedly one of the important reasons for the legal system reform in modern China. This is because there are profound historical differences between modern western legal culture and traditional Chinese legal culture. The former is closely connected with the commodity economic civilization system, while the latter is the inevitable legal manifestation of the natural economic civilization system. Therefore, the conflict between the two is inevitable. In this process, the superstitious faith in the eternity of the Celestial Empire broke down; the barbarous and hermetic isolation from the civilized world was infringed; and an opening was made for that intercourse which has since proceeded so rapidly under the golden attractions of California and Australia (Marx and Engels 1997: 2). However, it should be noted that this impact was limited after all, and the external impact could not be mystified. The impact of the West would eventually take effect through internal complex variables. For this reason, Chinese law has its inherent historical logic. Numerous literature analysis shows that the traditional Chinese legal culture based on natural economy, patriarchal relationship and autocratic regime developed to the beginning of the nineteenth century. Although there was no obvious change in quality, the ancient Chinese legal system had begun a slow process of change due to the changes in the internal economic and political conditions of the late Qing society. The Chinese legal system has a deep-rooted social foundation, cultural soil, and tough structure, so it is by no means easy to change its value orientation and legal system. Moreover, in the long history of thousands of years, the Chinese legal system has deeply affected all fields of ancient Chinese social life and restricted the legal consciousness of ancient Chinese people. However, a certain legal power relationship is a legal superstructure built on a certain socio-economic basis. When social and economic conditions change, the legal superstructure will inevitably change accordingly. Although the sprout of capitalism that had been bred during the Ming and Qing dynasties was ruthlessly strangled by the ruling group of the former Qing Empire, by the early nineteenth century, the commodity economy had grown tenaciously. After all, it played an increasingly important role in the social and economic system of the late Qing Dynasty compared with the previous dynasty. This provided conditions for the legal system reform in modern China.

It should be noted that giving full play to the autonomy, creativity and self-governing function of social subjects, maintaining the vitality and vitality of social progress, forming an endogenous force for the reform and development of the rule of law, and building an organic society ruled by law are one of the important objectives of the path of Chinese rule of law modernization. The modernization of the rule of law and the building of a society ruled by law are intrinsically combined. A country that has achieved rule of law modernization shall, on the whole, be a society ruled by law. The historic task of Chinese rule of law modernization is to realize the historic transformation to a society ruled by law. Therefore, a fundamental project to adhere to and expand the path of Chinese rule of law modernization is to accelerate the construction and formation of a society that believes in the rule of law and is ruled by law.

The realization of this goal and task is inseparable from the effective play of the active roles of various social subjects. The evolution of human civilization has continuously revealed and proved a profound and great truth: the birth of a new legal civilization is bound to be accompanied by the revolution of social subjects themselves. As the main social subject, people are the carrier of the value system of certain law. In the process of modernization of the rule of law, the degree of autonomy of social subjects is often the indicator of social anthropology to measure the development of the rule of law. For quite a long time after the founding of the People's Republic of China, a highly centralized planned economic system and a unified social control model have been built out of the objective existence of a certain level of social and economic development, which has suppressed the enthusiasm, initiative and creativity of social subjects. This situation is reflected in the process of the development of the rule of law, which is to emphasize the leading role of the government unilaterally, and ignore active roles of the social subject, which hinders the endogenous vitality of the development of society and the rule of law. The extensive development of the socialist market economy and the in-depth promotion of the socialist democratic politics have unprecedentedly stimulated the vitality of social life, effectively promoted the leap of social subjects itself engaged in this transformation, gradually established the autonomy of the social subject, and the pioneering spirit and intelligence of the social members have a broad space to fully exert. The characteristics of this era are reflected in the process of the development of the rule of law, which is reflected in the increasing proportion of social subject factors in the process of the development of the rule of law, and the social subject has increasingly become an important force to promote the reform and development of the rule of law. Therefore, the social endogenous evolution system of Chinese rule of law modernization has been gradually strengthened, and the construction of a society ruled by law has increasingly released its strong potential.

Since entering the new era of reform and opening up, *Deng Xiaoping* has regarded respecting the initiative of the people and mobilizing the enthusiasm of the people as one of the important goals and a basic experience of the political system reform, and regarded the people's belief or not, the people's promise or not, and the people's satisfaction or not as the basic yardstick to judge the success of the system, line and policy. Therefore, the most profound social factor or condition of Chinese rule of law modernization comes from the enthusiasm, initiative and pioneering spirit of the social subject. One of the basic requirements for advancing law-based governance across all fields of endeavor and accelerating the construction of a socialist country ruled by law is to confirm the broad social freedom of social subjects by using the authorized norms, give them broad social rights, stimulate the enthusiasm of social subjects to devote themselves to the cause of the rule of law and promote the development of the rule of law, and make it an inexhaustible source of power in the process of Chinese rule of law modernization.

In the new era of socialism with Chinese characteristics, the Party Central Committee with Comrade *Xi Jinping* as its core regards the development of whole-process people's democracy, the adherence to the people's principal position, and the orderly participation of citizens in democratic politics and the construction of the rule of law as an important principle in promoting Chinese rule of law modernization. Through various ways, mechanisms and methods, the Party Central Committee has taken the development of the people's democracy in the whole process, the adherence to the people's principal position, and the orderly participation of citizens in various fields such as grass-roots social autonomy, the right of the people to participate in the governance of the country and society is guaranteed according to law, the practice and exploration of grass-roots people in the reform of the rule of law are actively encouraged and fully respected, and the regional and grass-roots pilot of major reform measures of the rule of law are strengthened. The people have the right to know, participate, make decisions and supervise in the reform and development of the rule of law. This is the institutional advantage of the Chinese rule of law modernization, the fundamental difference between Chinese rule of law modernization and western rule of law modernization, and also reflects the bottom-up basic logic of the path of Chinese rule of law modernization. Therefore, the Decision of the Third Plenary Session of the 18th CPC Central Committee regards emancipating and enhancing social vitality as an important content of the guiding ideology of comprehensively deepening reform, and emphasizes that it is necessary to foster notions and form a business mechanism in conformity with the basic economic system in the primary stage of socialism and create a social environment in which people are encouraged to achieve something and helped to make a success of their career, so as to unleash all the vitality contained in work, knowledge, technology, management and capital and give full play to all sources of social wealth for the benefit of the people (China Institute of CPC Literature Research 2013).

The Decision of the Fourth Plenary Session of the 18th Central Committee of the Communist Party of China established upholding the people's principal position as one of the principles that must be followed to advance overall law-based governance, and put forward the major proposition that the people are the main body and source of strength of the rule of law, He stressed that the rule of law must be built for the people, rely on the people, benefit the people and protect the people (The CPC Central Committee 2014: 6). The 19th National Congress of the Communist Party of China stressed that The very purpose of developing socialist democracy is to give full expression to the will of the people, protect their rights and interests, spark their creativity, and provide systemic and institutional guarantees to ensure the people run the country. It pointed out that democracy is a common value of humanity and an ideal that has always been cherished by the CPC and the Chinese people. How to transform democratic values and concepts into scientific and effective institutional arrangements, and into concrete and realistic democratic practices, we need to pay attention to the organic unity of history and reality, theory and practice, form and content, and find the correct institutional mechanisms and methods (Xi 2022). We have achieved the unity of process democracy and result democracy, procedural democracy and substantive democracy, direct democracy and indirect democracy, people's democracy and the will of the state. It is a democracy that is all-chain, all-directional and all-inclusive, and is the most extensive, authentic and effective socialist democracy (Xi 2022). In the new era of socialism with Chinese characteristics, we should continue to promote the construction of people's democracy throughout the process, It has injected strong vitality into the development of a new path of Chinese rule of law modernization. Therefore, Xi (2021) further pointed out that China's socialist system ensures the position of the people as masters of the country. This is our institutional advantage and the fundamental difference between the rule of law in socialism with Chinese characteristics and the rule of law in capitalism. These important statements clearly reveal the main force of Chinese rule of law modernization and the basic orientation of its endogenous bottom-up social evolution, It points out the direction for adhering to and expanding the path of Chinese rule of law modernization.

On the other hand, it should be noted that from the perspective of the starting mechanism of the modernization of the rule of law in China, the active and effective promotion of the government often constitutes an important factor in starting the reform movement of the rule of law, and thus becomes a powerful driving force for promoting the modernization of the rule of law. Every legal reform movement in modern China depends on the promotion of appropriate types of government structures. The difference is that the value orientation of each type of political structure is different. The legal system reform movement in the late Qing Dynasty launched in the first ten years of the twentieth century shows that the role the government can play is limited when the imperial dynasty is facing a serious political crisis.

Over the 70 years since the founding of the People's Republic of China, especially the 40 years since the reform and opening up, contemporary Chinese society has entered a new historical stage, which has greatly liberated the social productive forces. However, in the process of transition to the new system, some noteworthy "anomie" phenomena have appeared in the process of social operation, and the authority of the government needs to be strengthened urgently. The issues of justice and efficiency in the implementation of the rule of law are more prominent, and the issue of social justice has not yet been effectively resolved. If this situation continues to develop, it will seriously hinder the smooth progress of the modernization of national governance, the reconstruction process of a good and effective social structure, and the effective development of Chinese modernization process of the rule of law, thus making this profound process of social and rule of law reform pay a heavy price. Therefore, when we strive to advance towards the goal of national modernization, choose and construct a new national functional model, we must proceed from the reality of our own country, fully consider the characteristics of our own country's economic, political, social and legal development, as well as our own national cultural background and historical tradition. Only a national functional model that is rooted in the national conditions of its own country and able to cope with various challenges is viable.

In face of the historic task of opening up a new path to the modernization of the rule of law in China, it was highlighted at the Decision of the Fourth Plenary Session of the 18th CPC Central Committee that the leadership of the Party provides the most fundamental guarantee for comprehensively advancing the law-based governance of China and accelerating the development of a socialist rule of law country. It is necessary to strengthen and improve the leadership of the Party in the work of the rule of law and implement the leadership of the Party into the whole process of advancing overall law-based governance. We need to strengthen institutions and work mechanisms for the law-based governance of China under the leadership of the Party; improve work mechanisms and procedures to ensure that the Party formulates principles, policies, and plans for the law-based governance of the country; strengthen unified leadership, unified planning, and overall coordination for comprehensively advancing the law-based governance of the country (China Institute of CPC Literature Research 2014).

The Resolution of the Sixth Plenary Session of the 19th Central Committee of the CPC profoundly summarized the historical experience of the Party's century-long struggle, and stressed that to govern our Party, which is the largest in the world, and our country, which is the most populous in the world, we must uphold the Party's overall leadership, especially the Central Committee's centralized, unified leadership, adhere to democratic centralism, and ensure that the Party exercises overall leadership and coordination (The CPC Central Committee 2021: 65). In contemporary China, the growing modern social mechanism and social main force provide a reliable social basis for promoting rule of law modernization, but only relying on the spontaneous evolution mechanism of society is far from meeting the practical needs of promoting Chinese rule of law modernization. Adhering to the overall leadership of the CPC in promoting the rule of law modernization and having a strong national capacity and a modern government system are crucial conditions for opening up and expanding a new path of Chinese rule of law modernization.

It can be seen that the process of promoting Chinese rule of law modernization clearly reflects the era character of two-way interaction from top to bottom and from bottom to top, and the organic unity of government promotion and social evolution. A distinctive feature of the way of promoting Chinese rule of law modernization is the internal interaction between the government and society. The path of Chinese rule of law modernization is the historical product of the interaction between government promotion and social evolution.

5.5 Conclusion

On the basis of a profound summary of the basic laws of the modernization of the rule of law in the world, President *Xi Jinping* has incisively outlined and elaborated three different types of ways to promote the modernization of the rule of law, namely, the social evolution model of promoting the modernization of the rule of law from the bottom-up, the government promotion model of promoting the modernization of the rule of law from the top-down, and the model of promoting the modernization of the rule of law by combining from the top-down and the bottom-up. The pattern of the rule of law modernization movement, which is interactive between government promotion and social evolution, as well as the two-way interaction between top-down and bottom-up rule of law modernization movement patterns, constitutes the prominent characteristics of ways of promoting Chinese rule of law modernization. For one thing, the profound impetus of the path of Chinese rule of law modernization comes from the powerful force of the rule of law reform generated by the endogenous evolution of the independent creative activities of the social subjects.

In contemporary China, the most profound source of motivation for promoting the modernization of the rule of law comes from the enthusiasm and initiative of social subjects and the broad participation of the people. The people are the active subject and source of strength of Chinese rule of law modernization. For another, the historical process of creating the path of Chinese rule of law modernization fully demonstrates that in contemporary China, building the rule of law in China and promoting Chinese rule of law modernization, there shall be a strong country that fully exercises its public management functions under the leadership of the CPC, and it shall ensure that the Party can effectively coordinate the work in all fields of law-based governance, and the will and propositions of the Party are carried out in law-based governance across all fields of endeavor. Since the 18th National Congress of the Communist Party of China, an obvious feature of promoting Chinese modernization of the rule of law is that the Party's strategic overall planning for advancing law-based governance across all fields of endeavor and the degree of its organization have been significantly and effectively improved, which has become a powerful driving force for the construction of the rule of law in China to expand in depth. As a result, a new model of promoting the Chinese rule of law modernization has been formed, which organically combines top-down and bottom-up, and promotes Chinese rule of law modernization through two-way interaction, thus making Chinese rule of law path full of vitality and vitality.

References

China Institute of CPC Literature Research. 2013. *Decision of the central committee of the communist party of China on several major issues concerning comprehensively deepening reform.* People's Publishing House.

China Institute of CPC Literature Research. 2014. *Decision of the central committee of the communist party of China on several major issues concerning comprehensively promoting the rule of law.* People's Publishing House.

Lawrence, M.F. 2019. *A history of American law.* Oxford University Press.

Marx, K., and Engels, F. 1956. *Complete works of Marx and Engels,* vol. 1. People's Publishing House.

Marx, K., and Engels, F. 1960. *Complete works of Marx and Engels*, vol. 3. People's Publishing House.

Marx, K., and Engels, F. 1997. *Marx and Engels on China*. People's Publishing House.

Marx, K., and Engels, F. 2009. *Collected works of Marx and Engels*, vol 10. People's Publishing House.

Max, W. 2012. *General economic history*. Dover Publications.

Michael, E.T. 2000. *Law and the rise of capitalism*. Monthly Review Press.

The Communist Party of China (CPC) Central Committee. 2021. *Resolution of the central committee of the communist party of China on the major achievements and historical experience of the Party over the past century*. People's Publishing House.

Xi, J. 2020. *On adhering to overall law-based governance of China*. Central Party Literature Press.

Xi, J. 2021. *People are the masters of the country*. Central Party Literature Press.

Xi, J. 2022. Speech at the working session of the central people's congress. *Qiu Shi*, 5.

Chapter 6
People-Oriented Nature of Chinese Thought on the Rule of Law

Abstract The people-oriented nature has become an important character of Chinese Thought on the Rule of Law. The people-oriented nature of Chinese Thought on the Rule of Law is formed on the basis of adhering to Marxism on the rule of law, inheriting and carrying forward the excellent traditional legal culture in China, etc. Its scientific connotation is embodied in upholding the people's principal position, protecting the people's legitimate rights and interests, relying on the people to promote the rule of law, adhering to the people's evaluation of the rule of law, etc. To show the people-oriented nature in the implementation of the rule of law, emphasis should be laid upon on sound legislation, strict law enforcement, impartial administration of justice, and observance of the law by everyone. The theoretical value of the people-oriented nature of Chinese Thought on Rule of Law lies in promoting the adaptation of Marxism on the Rule of Law to China's conditions, planning and coordinating all aspects of overall law-based governance, providing guidance for building a socialist country based on the rule of law, and contributing Chinese wisdom to the reform of global governance.

6.1 Introduction

Since the 18th National Congress of the Communist Party of China in 2012, General Secretary *Xi Jinping,* focusing on the themes of advancing overall law-based governance and striving to build China under the rule of law, has delivered a series of important speeches, which systematically and profoundly answered a series of major questions such as why and how to advance the overall law-based governance in the new era from the combination of theory and practice, forming Chinese Thought on Rule of Law characterized by rich content, strict logic, complete system and scientific elaboration. The people are the creators of history; they are the fundamental force that determines our Party and country's future (Xi 2017). Decrees may be followed if they are in accordance with the aspirations of the people; they may be ineffective if they are against the aspirations of the people (Xi 2014: 28). In the theoretical connotation of Chinese Thought on the Rule of Law, the people-oriented nature is

© The Author(s), under exclusive license to Springer Nature Singapore Pte Ltd. 2024
X. Dong and J. Guo, *Chinese Rule of Law Path and Cultivation of Foreign-Related Rule of Law Talents*, https://doi.org/10.1007/978-981-97-2313-3_6

one of the important characters, stemming from the fact that the people are the deep foundation of the CPC's governance as well as the starting point and foothold of the comprehensive law-based governance. At the Ceremony Marking the Centenary of the Communist Party of China, President *Xi Jinping* pointed out that this country is its people; the people are the country. As we have fought to establish and consolidate our leadership over the country, we have in fact been fighting to earn and keep the people's support. The Party has in the people its roots, its lifeblood, and its source of strength (Xi 2021a, b, c). Therefore, the people-oriented nature has become the fundamental character of Chinese Thought on the Rule of Law. Scholars attach great importance to the people-oriented nature of Chinese Thought on the Rule of Law, and believe that the people-oriented nature is the bright background of Chinese Thought on the Rule of Law (Chen and Qu 2021), the most distinctive character of Chinese Thought on the Rule of Law, the concrete embodiment of the philosophy of people-centered development in the field of the rule of law for a new era (Tang 2021), and an important part of Chinese Thought on the Rule of Law (Zhang 2021a, b).

The academic circles, on the basis of this consensus, have carried out a series of comprehensive and in-depth researches on Chinese Thought on the Rule of Law from the perspectives of the theoretical connotation, the mission of the rule of law and the implementation path. The first research perspective is from the theoretical connotation. The people-centered connotation in Chinese Thought on the Rule of Law includes upholding the principal position of the people, safeguarding the people's legitimate rights and interests, responding to the people's needs and living up to expectations, etc. (Hu 2021: 17). The people-centered position of the rule of law is mainly reflected in adhering to the rule of law for the people, adhering to the rule of law relying on the people, adhering to the rule of law to protect the people's rights and interests, etc. (Zhou 2021a, b: 43). Chinese Thought on the Rule of Law emphasizes the upholding of the principal position of the people, reflecting the people's will, safeguarding the people's interests and improving the people's well-being, which is a creative inheritance of the distinctive character of the people-oriented nature in Marxism in China for a new era (Sun 2021) and the third historical leap in the Sinicization of Marxist jurisprudence (Zhang 2021a, b). The second research perspective is from the mission of the rule of law. The mission of the rule of law is an important theme of Chinese Thought on the Rule of Law. The socialist rule of law with Chinese characteristics carries the important mission of protecting the rights and interests of the people (Yu 2021a, b). The fundamental position of adhering to the people-centered Chinese Thought on the Rule of Law should be implemented in the whole process of the overall law-based governance (Yu 2021a, b: 16), and the people-centered nature of justice should be highlighted closely around the important requirement of "strive to make the people see in every judicial case that justice is served" (Cui 2021).The third research perspective is from the the implementation path. To implement Chinese Thought on the Rule of Law, we need to grasp the value pursuit of social fairness and justice (Zhou 2021a, b), and strive to give full play to the main responsibility of leading cadres and the mainstay of political and legal team (Fu 2021).

The above-mentioned interpretation has deepened the theoretical understanding and expanded the theoretical vision of the people-oriented nature of Chinese Thought on the Rule of Law, and further put forward the problems worthy of systematic thinking from the micro level: what is the logic to form the people-oriented nature of Chinese Thought on the Rule of Law? What are the main aspects of the scientific connotation of the people-oriented nature of Chinese Thought on the Rule of Law based on the formation logic? How to implement the people-oriented nature of Chinese Thought on the Rule of Law? What are its contributions to the theory of socialist rule of law with Chinese characteristics? With these questions in, this chapter, based on the above research, intends to analyze the people-oriented nature of Chinese Thought on the Rule of Law from four aspects: formation logic, scientific connotation, implementation path and theoretical value, in order to further deepen and expand the research of Chinese Thought on the Rule of Law.

6.2 Formation Logic

1. Theoretical Logic

The formation of any thought is a process of drawing beneficial elements on the basis of predecessors and continuing to mature in specific practice. As the latest theoretical achievement of "thinking and guiding the rule of law in China with the general principles of Marxism", Chinese Thought on the Rule of Law has a solid logical foundation of theory (Sun 2021), which is based on the legal thoughts of classical Marxist writers and the constructive achievements of western legal civilization.

The first is the rule of law thought of classical Marxist writers. In the history of human thought, no theory has had such a broad and profound impact on mankind as Marxism (Xi 2018). Marxism emphasizes that the only creator of material and spiritual wealth in the society is the people. Therefore, the only support for the continuous operation of the wheel of history is also the people (Jin 2022: 65). *Marx* and *Engels* believe that the implementation of law is to serve the people. Certainty can only exist if the law is the conscious expression of the popular will, and therefore originates with it and is created by it (Marx and Engels 2010: 309). There are a great number of incisive discussions around the people's position, interests and evaluation standards in *Lenin Collected Works*, which fully demonstrate Lenin's sincere and profound care for the people and the value pursuit of "putting the people first". Marxist classical writers provide a theoretical source for the people-oriented nature of Chinese Thought on the Rule of Law. President *Xi Jinping* pointed out that the people-oriented nature is the most distinctive character of Marxism (Xi 2019: 429). In November 2020, at the Central Working Conference on the Comprehensive Law-based Governance, President *Xi Jinping* emphasized and deployed "adhering to the people as the center" as a key work that must be done well to further promote the comprehensive law-based governance at present and in the future. Since the 18th National Congress of the Communist Party of China, the Party Central Committee with Comrade *Xi Jinping* as the core has always adhered to the general principles of Marxism to guide the construction of the rule of law in China, upheld the principal position of the people, and creatively inherited Marxism on the Rule of Law, such as materiality, politics, people, sociality, practicality and inheritance (Sun 2021). As a new development and new leap in the Sinicization of Marxism on the Rule of Law, Chinese Thought on the Rule of Law adheres to the fundamental position of the people, emphasizes the firm standing with the people, implementation of the Party's mass line, respect for the people's creativity, as well as the development of the people-centered philosophy, and highlights that the overall law-based governance must uphold the principal position of the people, and the in-depth promotion of the overall law-based governance must adhere to the people as the center.

The second is constructive achievements of Western civilization of the rule of law. Although the rule of law in western countries is different from that in China in terms of regime and economic and social development, the rule of law in China in the new era can take the essence and discard the dregs of Western rule of law. First of all, the core spirit of Western rule of law is justice. *Aristotle* believes that equality and justice are the essence of justice. German jurist *Radbruch* mentioned that justice is equal, while *Yelin* pointed out that justice is security. China has also reasonably absorbed and learned from the core spirit of justice in the construction of the rule of law. Secondly, the rule of law is more advantageous than the rule of man. According to the Western Thought on the rule of law, the effects of rule of law are better than those of rule of man. Thirdly, an important issue of legal theory is "belief in law", which plays a decisive role in the realization of the value of law and affects the promotion of the rule of law. *Rousseau* (1994: 89) mentioned in *Discourse on Political Economy and the Social Contract* that the most important law in all laws is not engraved on marble or bronze watches, but in the hearts of citizens. *Harold J. Berman* (1974: 16), a famous contemporary American jurist, once said that only when people fully believe in the law can the law really play a binding role in society. It is impossible to believe in the law overnight. It needs the constraints of the external environment and the sincere respect from the bottom of the heart. It also needs the society to optimize the environment of the rule of law continuously. Constructive achievements of Western legal civilization provides important ideas for accelerating the construction of the rule of law. We should have faith in and awe of the law, and ensure that the whole people abide by the law, internalize it in hearts and externalize it in actions. It can be said that the people-oriented nature in Chinese Thought on the Rule of Law has absorbed the essence of excellent rule of law civilization in the world, proceeded from the reality of China, and explored the path of rule of law that is suitable for China's national conditions in the practice of construction and reform.

2. Historical Logic

At the Ceremony Marking the Centenary of the Communist Party of China, *Xi Jinping* profoundly pointed out that since the very day of its founding, the Party has made seeking happiness for the Chinese people and rejuvenation for the Chinese nation its aspiration and mission (Xi 2021a, b, c). The people-oriented nature of Chinese Thought on the Rule of Law is formed on the basis of inheriting the concept that people are the foundation of a state in the traditional legal culture and unremitting pursuit of the CPC's leadership of the construction of rule of law.

The first is the concept that people are the foundation of a state. During the Shang and Zhou dynasties, the people-centered philosophy had not formed a complete system, but it can still be seen from the historical process that ordinary people played an important role in the rise and fall of a country. Just as the old saying in Shoo King, "The people should be cherished, and not looked down upon. The people are the root of a country. The root firm, the country is tranquil." During the Spring and Autumn period and the Warring States period, Confucianism, Legalism, Taoism and Mohism had far-reaching impacts on the thought of the rule of law. In terms of the concept that people are the foundation of a state, *Confucius* and *Mencius* advocated the implementation of "benevolent governance", paying attention to "rule by man", "rule by virtue" and "rule by rites" and putting the people in the primary position and themselves in the secondary position. The legalists represented by *Shang Yang* and *Han Fei* discussed the origin, nature, function and social relationship of law and advocated the rule of law. After the unification of the Six Kingdoms in the Qin Dynasty, Confucian classics were regarded as orthodoxy, and Chinese feudal law began to be Confucianism. During the Han and Tang Dynasties, with the economic prosperity and development, the concept that people are the foundation of a state developed to a new height and became an orthodox ideology. In the Ming and Qing Dynasties, the concept that people are the foundation of a state developed toward perfection. *Zhang Juzheng*, a politician in the Ming Dynasty, believes that "pacifying, benefiting and supporting the people" is the way to govern. *Su Shi*, a well known writer in the Northern Song Dynasty, once said that getting rid of the scourge of the common people is like getting rid of my own heart disease, which means that we should love the people as sons and solve the people's problems just like getting rid of our own heart disease. These thoughts all reflect the profound concept that people are the foundation of a state. President *Xi Jinping* inherited the value orientation of "being close to the people and loving the people" in the concept that people are the foundation of a state, believed "the people's livelihood matters most of all things", and added new connotation to it in the process of the times, showing a distinct people-oriented nature.

The second is the thought on the rule of law of successive leaders of the Communist Party of China. China's development is inseparable from the hard work and struggle of the broad masses of the people as well as the efforts and exploration of the leaders of the Communist Party of China. Since the founding of the People's Republic of China, Comrade *Mao Zedong* combined the basic theory of Marxism with China's specific revolution and construction and explored the theoretical direction and specific practice of the legal construction of new China with great courage. Comrade *Mao Zedong* (1991: 1301) pointed out that the masses are the masters of history, only the people, to create the driving force of world history. In the new period of reform and opening up, the Chinese Communists represented by Comrade *Deng Xiaoping* (1994: 146) have a deeper understanding of the relationship between democracy and the legal system: in order to protect people's democracy, we must strengthen the legal system, and democracy and legal system should be upheld.

They are like two hands, and neither hand can be weakened. Comrade *Jiang Zemin* stressed the need to strengthen the construction of socialist democratic politics, but also the construction of socialist legal system. In 1996, in the concluding speech of the third lecture on Legal System of the CPC Central Committee, Comrade *Jiang Zemin* put forward the strategy of the law-based governance and comprehensively and profoundly expounded the great significance of the law-based governance. With the advent of the new century, Comrade *Hu Jintao* put forward the Scientific Outlook on Development, requiring China's development and construction to emphasize the people-centered philosophy, establishing the concept of comprehensive and sustainable development, and realizing the all-round development of economy, society and people at the same time. These important expositions have profoundly expounded the basic truth that socialist democracy needs the guarantee of socialist rule of law and pointed out the basic path of synchronously promoting the construction of socialist democracy and rule of law under the leadership of the Party. Socialism with Chinese characteristics has entered a new era, and the construction of socialist democracy and the rule of law has opened a new chapter. President *Xi Jinping* (2020: 92) pointed out the organic unity of adhering to the Party's leadership, the people being the masters of the country and the law-based governance is a basic experience of China's socialist rule of law construction. In China, the key to developing socialist democratic politics, ensuring that it is our people who run the country and guaranteeing that the country's political life is dynamic, stable and orderly is to adhere to the organic unity of the Party's leadership, the people being the masters of the country and the law-based governance. President *Xi Jinping* (2022) also spoke highly of the strength and role of the people. He stressed on different occasions that the people are the true heroes, for it is they who create history (Xi 2016a, b), and the great achievements of the new era have come from the collective dedication and hard work of our Party and our people (Xi 2022). These important expositions are an important embodiment of the people-oriented nature of Chinese Thought on the Rule of Law and the crystallization of the wisdom of the new generation of Chinese Communists to carry forward the past and forge ahead into the future, unite and lead the people of the whole country to deeply promote the comprehensive law-based governance and unremittingly pursue the rule of law for the people.

6.3 Scientific Connotation

The relationship between the rule of law and the people is a basic issue in the overall law-based governance, which is related to the basic position and development direction of the socialist rule of law. The Party Central Committee with Comrade *Xi Jinping* as the core firmly adhered to the people's position of socialist rule of law, closely focused on the multi-dimensional relationship between rule of law construction and people's position, rights and interests, feelings and strength, and comprehensively and deeply answered the basic questions of the overall law-based governance, such as value subject, evaluation criteria and source of strength, so as to systematically show the scientific connotation of the people-oriented nature of Chinese Thought on the Rule of Law.

1. Upholding the Principal Position of the People

The people exist not only as the main body in the construction of the rule of law, but also as the backbone of the construction of China under the rule of law. In building the rule of law in a socialist country where the people are the masters of the country, it is imperative to always bear in mind the people's position and uphold the principal position of the people, which is the primary embodiment of the people-oriented nature of Chinese Thought on the Rule of Law. Upholding the principal position of the people means that Party members and cadres stand on the people's side, take the people as the starting point in what they think and do, and resolutely represent and safeguard the fundamental interests of the people. President *Xi Jinping* (2020: 107) pointed out that China's socialist system ensures the principal position of the people as masters of the country and the principal position of the people in the comprehensive law-based governance, which is our institutional advantage and the fundamental reason why the socialist rule of law with Chinese characteristics is different from the capitalist rule of law. Therefore, in deepening the work of the comprehensive law-based governance, it is essential to uphold the principal position of the people, grasp the key of the people's principal position in the constitution, adhere to the organic unity of the Party's leadership, the people being the masters of the country and the comprehensive law-based governance, carry forward people's democracy, pool the people's wisdom and reflect the common will of all the people. As the fundamental law of the country, the socialist system and people's Congress system determined by China's constitution are the concentrated embodiment of the constitutional concept that all power belongs to the people in China at the level of legal system. President *Xi Jinping* stressed on many important occasions that adhering to the state system of the people's democratic dictatorship and the political system of the people's Congress system determined by the constitution is an inherent requirement for upholding the people's principal position and adhering to the constitutional concept that all power of the state belongs to the people in the in-depth promotion of the comprehensive law-based governance in the new era. These important expositions have profoundly expounded the supreme principal states of the people in China's socialist system and socialist rule of law.

2. Protecting the Legitimate Rights and Interests of the People

An important connotation of Chinese Thought on the Rule of Law is to protect the legitimate rights and interests of the people. President *Xi Jinping* (2021) stressed that the fundamental purpose of promoting the comprehensive law-based governance is to protect the rights and interests of the people according to law. The rule of law has an important function of protecting rights, and protecting people's rights and interests is an important mission of the socialist rule of law with Chinese characteristics (Yu 2021a, b). To adhere to the people-oriented nature in further promoting the comprehensive law-based governance is to give full play to the right protection function of the rule of law, so as to better protect the legitimate rights and interests of the people. In the construction and practice of the rule of law, it is very important for leading cadres at all levels to protect the legitimate rights and interests of the people. President *Xi Jinping* (2020: 135) pointed out that the specific exercise of the Party's ruling power and the state's legislative, administrative, supervisory and judicial power by leading cadres is the key to the comprehensive law-based governance, the Party's leadership in legislation, ensuring law enforcement, supporting justice and taking the lead in abiding by the law is mainly reflected and realized through the specific actions and work of leading cadres at all levels. Therefore, since the 18th CPC National Congress, the Party Central Committee with Comrade *Xi Jinping* as the core has paid special attention to the importance of leading cadres taking the lead in respecting the law, learning about the law and abiding by the law for further promoting the comprehensive law-based governance and protecting the legitimate rights and interests of the people. The Party Central Committee with Comrade *Xi Jinping* as the core focuses on solving problems in practice, and emphasizes that leading cadres should adhere to the bottom line of the rule of law, take the lead in respecting and abiding by the law, which fully shows the people-oriented nature of Chinese Thought on the rule of law and deeply expounds the importance of leading cadres' strict implementation of the rule of law to protect the legitimate rights and interests of the people.

3. Relying on the People to Promote the Rule of Law

Relying on the people to promote the construction of the rule of law is an important embodiment of the people-oriented nature of Chinese Thought on the Rule of Law. The most extensive and profound foundation for the comprehensive law-based governance is the people, so it is of paramount importance to adhere to serving and relying on the people. The cause of socialist rule of law with Chinese characteristics in the new era must closely rely on the joint efforts of the broad masses of the people. President *Xi Jinping* (2020: 107) pointed out the necessity to fully mobilize the enthusiasm and initiative of the people to devote themselves to the practice of governing the country according to law. Under the guidance of Chinese Thought on the Rule of Law, the Implementation Outline for the Construction of A Society Based on Rule of Law (2020–2025) issued by the CPC Central Committee in December 2020 stressed that we should cultivate the belief in the rule of law in the whole society, enhance the pertinence and effectiveness of publicity and education on the rule of law, guide all the people to be loyal advocates, conscientious adherents and firm defenders of the socialist rule of law, and make the rule of law a social consensus and basic principle (CPC Central Committee 2020). The Plan for the Construction of China Based on the Rule of Law (2020–2025), issued by the CPC Central Committee in January 2021, emphasizes and deploys to promote the comprehensive law-based governance by relying on the people (CPC Central Committee 2021). These important decisions are of guiding significance to better organize and mobilize the people of the whole country and concentrate on the construction of socialist rule of law under the new historical conditions. In modern society, the rule of law is an important support for national governance, and the modernization of the rule of law is a cause that needs to be promoted synchronously and harmoniously with the modernization of national governance. The modernization of the rule of law is a far-reaching transformation process including the transformation of legal system, legal value and rule of law culture (Zhang 2021a, b). In the new era of high-quality economic and social development, to actively and steadily promote the modernization of the rule of law and ensure that the construction of the rule of law can meet the practical requirements of economic and social development and the modernization of national governance, it is urgent to fully stimulate the enthusiasm of all the people to respect the rule of law under the centralized and unified leadership of the Party Central Committee, give full play to positive roles of the broad masses of the people in consciously participating in the construction of socialist rule of law.

4. Adhering to the People's Evaluation on the Rule of Law

The evaluation criteria of the rule of law will be different due to different evaluation subjects, so it has subjectivity (Luo 2021: 130). In socialist China, the people are the main body of overall law-based governance and the assessors of the construction of the rule of law. The effectiveness of the construction of the rule of law should ultimately be assessed and evaluated by the people (Zhou 2021a, b). The people are the supreme arbiter and final judge of our Party's work (Xi 2014). President *Xi Jinping* stressed the need to take the people's support, approval, satisfaction and consent as the fundamental standards to measure the gains and losses of all work (Wang et al. 2021) and strive to make the people feel fairness and justice in every legal system, every law enforcement decision and every judicial case (Xi 2020). It is required to fully respect the people's inner feelings of fairness and justice and pay full attention to the people's sense of rule of law in deepening the practice of the overall law-based governance. The fairness and justice of the rule of law is not only to enable professional personage of the rule of law to enjoy fairness and justice, but also to enable people to enjoy fairness and justice. The rule of law is the cause of good governance, and good law is the foundation of good governance. With the continuous improvement of the socialist legal system with Chinese characteristics with the *Constitution* as the core, it has been realized that there are laws to abide by in all aspects of our national and social life on the whole. In this legislative context, the focus of the people's attention to legislation is no longer "establishing a law in order to have a law to rely on", but "establishing a good law in order to have a good law and good governance". The expectation of the people for legislation is not whether there is any, but whether it is good or not, whether it works or not, and whether it can solve practical problems; not all laws can govern the country, not all laws can govern the country well; the more emphasis on the rule of law, the more it is necessary to improve the quality of legislation (Marx and Engels 2010: 20). The real experience of the people themselves is the most convincing criterion to evaluate the effects of the construction of the rule of law. These important expositions, from the perspective of the subject of the evaluation of the rule of law, deeply show the people-oriented nature of Chinese Thought on the Rule of Law and are the creative interpretation and application of the principle of the people-oriented nature of Marxism on the Rule of Law in the construction of China's rule of law in the new era.

6.4 Implementation Path

Since the 18th CPC National Congress, the CPC Central Committee has laid emphasis on the construction of the rule of law and made continuous theoretical and practical breakthroughs. President *Xi Jinping* expressed his implementation opinions on further integrating socialist core values into the construction of the rule of law: adhering to the combination of the law-based governance and the virtue-based governance, integrating the core socialist values into the whole process of building a country based on the rule of law, a government based on the rule of law and a society based on the rule of law, and integrating them into all links of sound legislation, strict law enforcement, impartial administration of justice, and observance of law by everyone (Xi 2016a, b). Among them, the people-oriented nature is the essence of Chinese Thought on the rule of law, which has solid practical value. The implementation path is mainly carried out under the guidance of sound legislation, strict law enforcement, impartial administration of justice, and observance of law by everyone.

1. Committing to the People-centered Approach in Sound Legislation

Legislation is the primary link of the rule of law, so paying attention to legislation means paying attention to the source. The Fourth Plenary Session of the 18th CPC Central Committee stressed the necessity to pay attention to legislative work, achieve the combination of democracy and science in the specific legislative process, reflect the people's substantive demands, and gain the people's support and belief. Strengthening democratic legislation is the internal requirement and important aspect of promoting the construction of socialist rule of law by developing people's democracy in the whole process. Only when the law is the conscious expression of the people's will and is made with the people's will and created by the people's will, can a definite grasp be ensured (Xi 2020). Firstly, speed up and improve the communication mechanism. In the construction of socialist rule of law with Chinese characteristics, strengthening democratic legislation as well as enhancing legislative democracy and public participation will help fully absorb the will of the people, promote the construction of a complete legal system, and lay a solid legislative foundation for China with good law and good governance based on the rule of law. To this end, efforts should be made to improve the mechanism for soliciting opinions on legislation, expand the coverage and representativeness of public participation, and enhance the transparency of legislation. Explanations should be given to those relatively concentrated opinions that have not been adopted (CPC Central Committee 2021). Secondly, improve the platform and carrier of democratic public opinion expression of the National People's Congress. It is highly recommended that new media and new technologies be used actively to expand the channels of public participation in legislation, and improve the mechanism of legislative hearing and public opinion survey (CPC Central Committee 2021), the working mechanism of absorbing public opinion be improved, the wisdom of the people be taken advantage of, and the social situation and public opinion of all aspects into the fundamental interests of the overwhelming majority of the people be integrated (Xi 2021a, b, c). Thirdly, give full play to the role of deputies to the National People's Congress. Deputies to the National

People's Congress are the "spokesmen" of the people. In the process of long-term practice and exploration, many effective forms for deputies to the National People's Congress to participate in legislation have been formed gradually. At the same time, it is necessary to innovate and improve the mechanism for deputies to the National People's Congress at all levels to participate in legislation and give more play to the role of deputies to the National People's Congress in drafting and amending laws.

2. Serving the People in Strict Law Enforcement

Strictness is the premise and foundation for the orderly operation of society and the guarantee of authority and credibility. Strict law enforcement is to strictly abide by the rules within the framework of the *Constitution* and laws, so as to be fair and strict. President *Xi Jinping* (2020: 96) believes that the vitality of law lies in implementation, and the authority of law also lies in implementation. Law is the concentrated embodiment of the people's will. To promote and ensure the effective implementation of the law through supervision is to promote and ensure the realization of the people's will according to the law. Only by taking the people's will as the center and strengthening the supervision of law implementation, can the people's will contained in legislation be fully realized in specific law implementation activities. Firstly, law enforcers must establish the concept of law enforcement for the people. Law enforcers are the staff of state organs and the representatives of public power, but their power is given by the people and should naturally serve the people. The rights of the people matter most, so strict law enforcement requires law enforcers to put the vital interests of the people first, consciously safeguard the rights and interests of the people, and create a good legal environment for the people. Secondly, professional ethics should be abided by strictly. Law enforcers should establish correct professional ideals, act according to industry norms, listen to the opinions of the people, understand the needs of the people, and truly enforce the law for the people. Thirdly, law enforcers are the executors and enforcers of the law. A good way of thinking on the rule of law should be developed to improve the level of law enforcement, improve the credibility of national law enforcement organs, and make law enforcers and law enforcement departments the most reliable dependence of the broad masses of the people.

3. Putting the People First in Impartial Administration of Justice

Justice is an important means to safeguard national security, public security and social order and good customs. It is the last line of defense and relief mechanism to protect human rights (Liu 2021). To achieve impartial administration of justice and ensure that judicial work in China can uphold the people as the core, the specific implementation path of impartial justice can be started from the following three aspects. Firstly, ensure that the judiciary exercises its power independently and impartially and meet the expectations of the people. For one thing, the administration and localization of judicial power must be removed, which requires all provinces in China to strengthen the full integration of various resources of judicial organs, especially in the aspect of judicial funds. For another, the relationship between fair justice and the public should be effectively coordinated. It is the starting point of the work of judicial organs to fully understand the needs and wishes of the broad masses of the people, increase the depth of the broad masses of the people's participation in judicial work, and protect the broad masses of the people's enthusiasm for judicial work. Secondly, deepen the reform of the judicial responsibility system and safeguard the rights and interests of the people. For one thing, the profound relationship between the Party's leadership and the reform of judicial responsibility system should be understood. Judicial work should accept the Party's leadership, and the people's court must strengthen the reform and implementation of judicial responsibility system, ensure the correct direction of the reform of the judicial responsibility system, guarantee the independence and fairness of the people's courts in exercising judicial power, strengthen the construction of a clean government and fight corruption in China's judicial organs. For another, the relationship between decentralization and supervision should be handled correctly. To make justice public is to let the broad masses of the people know relevant information. Thirdly, a complete restriction and supervision system should be built. External supervision mainly depends on the active participation of the broad masses of the people and the broadened channels and methods of supervision. People's courts at all levels may elect a group of representatives from legal scholars, CPPCC members, journalists, lawyers, enterprises and community residents to conduct judicial supervision, combine traditional supervision methods with new media platforms, and strengthen the publicity of procuratorial work and the openness of procuratorial affairs.

4. Enhancing the Concept of Equality in Observance of Law by Everyone

The Observance of law by everyone should not be the last key to overall law-based governance in China, but should fully reflect the concept of the observance of the law by everyone in the process of legislation and law enforcement (Ying 2020). President *Xi Jinping* believes that the Party and the government's strategy of overall law-based governance must fully reflect the principal position of the people. To guide the participation of the broad masses of the people, it is necessary to create a good law enforcement and law-abiding social atmosphere. This fully shows that only when the law is revered and respected by the people can it exert its maximum force. The specific implementation path of the observance of the law by everyone can be started from the following three aspects. Firstly, implement the work of popularizing the law among the whole people and establish the concept of equality. In the process of promoting law popularization, excellent deeds and models should be discovered to encourage the people to keep up with these models. At the same time, the participation mechanism in law popularization should be broadened to enrich law popularization resources and expand the scope of law popularization. Meanwhile, on the basis of traditional news communication carriers, new forms should be explored to make full use of the communication role of mobile phones, the Internet, television and other media. Secondly, implement the punishment and reward system to enhance public awareness of the rule of law. A mechanism for dishonest behavior has been established to severely punish the seriously dishonest behavior of market subjects, and to improve personal credit records. The major theoretical viewpoints on the issues of the relationship between morality and law, the basis of major reform in the law and the legalization of social governance in Chinese Thought on the Rule of Law have been comprehensively implemented into the process of the construction of social credit system to promote the legalization of social credit system, and then serve the improvement of social governance standard system and the modernization of social governance (Tan and Liu 2021).

6.5 Theoretical Value

As the largest developing country, under the guidance of Chinese Thought on the Rule of Law, China adheres to the development of people-centered philosophy and promotes the modernization of national governance system and governance capacity. In this sense, there are a great number of theoretical values in Chinese Thought on the Rule of Law with the distinctive characteristics of the people-oriented nature.

1. Providing the Latest Achievements for Marxism to Adapt to China's Conditions

Chinese Thought on the Rule of Law provides the latest achievements for Marxism on the Rule of Law to adapt to China's conditions. Chinese Thought on the Rule of Law is based on China's reality, starting from China's practice of rule of law, endows Marxism on the rule of law with the significance of the times and creatively enriches the people-oriented nature of Marxism on the Rule of Law. At the fundamental level, the capability of our Party and the strengths of socialism with Chinese characteristics are attributable to the fact that Marxism works (Xi 2021a, b, c). The people-oriented nature is the most distinctive character of Marxism and the most distinctive character of Marxism on the Rule of Law. In the centennial process of adaptation of Marxism on the Rule of Law to the China's Conditions, the Chinese Communists founded Mao Zedong Legal Thought, the Theory of Socialist Rule of Law with Chinese Characteristics, and Chinese Thought on the Rule of Law, realizing three historic leaps in the adaptation of Marxism on the Rule of Law to China's conditions (Zhang 2021a, b). The people-oriented nature of Chinese Thought on the Rule of Law is not a simple restatement of the people-oriented nature advocated by the classical Marxist writers but is generated by combining the Marxism with China's conditions of the construction of the rule of law since the 18th CPC National Congress, which has the excellent character of keeping pace with the times in theory and practice. As the theoretical achievement of the third historic leap in the Sinicization of Marxism on the Rule of Law, Chinese Thought on the Rule of Law, upholding that the principal position of the people is deeply rooted in the people, fully embodies the will of the people and firmly protects the interests of the people (Sun 2021), consolidates the principal position of the people in overall law-based governance and improves the value contribution of the thought of the rule of law, which provides the people-centered basic position, viewpoint and method for further promoting overall law-based governance in the new era and lays a solid foundation for Chinese Thought on the Rule of Law to become the latest achievement of for Marxism to adapt to China's conditions.

2. Providing Guidance for Promoting the Overall Law-based Governance

As the core of Chinese Thought on the Rule of Law, the people-oriented nature provides value guidance for coordinating all aspects of the relationship of the overall law-based governance. Overall law-based governance must correctly handle the relationship between politics and the rule of law, reform and the rule of law, the law-based governance and the virtue-based governance (Party Literature Research Office of the CPC Central Committee 2015: 34). Take the correct understanding and handling of the relationship between politics and the rule of law as an example, politics and the rule of law are both superstructure categories, which complement each other and are inseparable. There is politics in the rule of law, and there is no rule of law divorced from politics. There is a set of political theory behind every form of rule of law, there is a political logic in every model of rule of law, and there is a political position under every road of rule of law (Party Literature Research Office of the CPC Central Committee 2015: 34). In China, the key to dealing with the relationship between politics and the rule of law is to deal with the relationship between the Party and the law. The relationship between the Party and the law is a concentrated reflection of the relationship between politics and the rule of law. The relationship between the Party and the law is a fundamental problem. If it is handled well, the rule of law, the Party and the country will prosper; if it is not handled well, the rule of law, the Party and the country will decline (Party Literature Research Office of the CPC Central Committee 2015: 33). Chinese Thought on the Rule of Law not only fully reflects the people-oriented nature of the Party and the law, but also makes the people as the axis in coordinating the relationship between politics and the rule of law. Taking the people-oriented nature of Chinese Thought on the Rule of Law as the value index to guide and coordinate the relationship between politics and the rule of law is conducive to actively and steadily promoting the construction of socialist rule of law. Actively and steadily promoting the construction of socialist rule of law is conducive to strengthening and improving the Party's leadership by taking advantage of the mode of rule of law, so as to improve the Party's ability and level of ruling according to law, make the Party's leadership more stable and far-reaching, which in turn provides a more fundamental, stable and long-term political guarantee for the construction of socialist rule of law, forms a benign interaction between the Party's leadership and overall law-based governance to ensure the long-term stability of the Party and the country and truly benefit the people.

3. Providing Directions for Building a Socialist Country Based on the Rule of Law

Since the 18th CPC National Congress, Chinese Thought of Socialism with Chinese Characteristics for a new era has provided a powerful ideological weapon for realizing modernization of Chinese style (Xi 2021a, b, c). The people-oriented nature is the distinct characteristic of Chinese Thought on the Rule of Law, and it is also the core idea of Chinese Thought on Socialism with Chinese Characteristics for a new era. As a major theoretical innovation that meets the requirements of the great rejuvenation of the Chinese nation, Chinese Thought on the Rule of Law has important guiding significance for the Party to lead the people of the whole country to promote high-quality development and realize high-quality life under the guidance of the rule of law at a new historical starting point. On the new journey of building a modern socialist country in an all-round way, a key point to give better play to the role of the rule of law in consolidating the foundation, stabilizing expectations and benefiting the long-term development is to always adhere to the people-centered concept of the rule of law and implement Chinese Thought on the Rule of Law, so as to provide a strong rule of law guarantee for the overall layout of coordinated implementation of the five-sphere integrated plan and the four-pronged comprehensive strategy, provide more satisfactory products of the rule of law for the well-being of the people and the stability of society in modern socialist countries, make the people have more sense of fulfillment, happiness and security, and ensure the smooth construction of a prosperous, strong, democratic, civilized, harmonious and beautiful modern socialist country in the middle of this century.

4. Contributing Chinese Wisdom to the Reform of Global Governance

Chinese Thought on the Rule of Law contributes Chinese wisdom to the construction of the rule of law for all mankind and the reform of global governance. The Party Central Committee with Comrade *Xi Jinping* as the core, starting from the great changes that have not occurred in the world in a century, scientifically answers the questions of the times that "what's wrong with the world, what should we do and what can be done by the rule of law", which is the Chinese wisdom that contributes to the construction of the rule of law and the reform of global governance. President *Xi Jinping* once said, why can our reform and development be carried out in an orderly manner and the society maintain long-term stability? A very important factor is that we always adhere to the people-centered development philosophy, take the promotion of social fairness and justice and the improvement of people's well-being as the starting point and foothold of our work, and strive to make the people have more sense of fulfillment, happiness and security (Xi 2020). This is a concentrated summary of China's development experience. The essence of this experience is to base on national conditions, uphold the people's principal position, and put the people first. Adhering to the people-centered Chinese Thought on the Rule of Law featured by the people-oriented nature has not only made remarkable achievements and accumulated valuable experience in solving China's development and governance problems, but also has reference significance for other developing countries to solve their own development and governance problems. In the face of the ever-changing international situation, under the guidance of the concept of a global community of shared future for mankind, how to base ourselves on our country, look to the world, play the role of a major and responsible country, take advantage of the rule of law to benefit the people of all countries and promote the reform of global governance is a major rule of law issue in today's world. President *Xi Jinping* pointed out promoting the construction of "the Belt and Road" needs the protection of the rule of law. China wants to create a good environment of the rule of law, build a fair, reasonable and transparent international economic and trade system with other countries, so as to promote the high quality development of "the Belt and Road", and better benefit the people of all countries (Xi 2020: 268). The Party will continue to work with all peace-loving countries and peoples to promote the shared human values of peace, development, fairness, justice, democracy, and freedom (Xi 2021a, b, c). It is with such a global concept and the responsibility of a big country that China linked the construction of domestic rule of law with the development of the interests of the people of the world, and worked with the people of all countries to promote the construction of "the Belt and Road" and a global community of shared future, which is a true demonstration of the people-oriented nature of Chinese Thought on the Rule of Law in the international community.

6.6 Conclusion

The people-oriented nature is the theoretical essence and essence of Chinese Thought on the Rule of Law. The people-oriented nature of Chinese Thought on the Rule of Law comes from firmly adhering to the people-oriented nature of Marxism on the Rule of Law, unremitting pursuit of the original intention of the Communist Party of China to lead the construction of the rule of law and inheriting and carrying forward the concept that people are the foundation of a state. The people-oriented nature of Chinese Thought on the Rule of Law has been fully reflected by upholding the people's principal position, protecting the people's legitimate rights and interests, relying on the people to promote the rule of law, and adhering to the people's evaluation of the effectiveness of the rule of law construction, which systematically answers the basic questions of the value subject, right orientation, evaluation criteria and source of strength of overall law-based governance. Therefore, in the process of further promoting the work of overall law-based governance, to show and practice the people-oriented nature of Chinese Thought on the Rule of Law, efforts should be made to focus on the people-centered approach in sound legislation, serve the people in strict law enforcement, put the people first in impartial administration of justice, and enhance the concept of equality in observance of law by everyone. There is an important guiding significance of the people-oriented nature of Chinese Thought on the Rule of Law in providing the latest achievements for Marxism to adapt to China's conditions, providing guidance for the overall planning and coordination of all aspects of overall law-based governance.

References

Chen, J., & Qu, Z. (2011, January 11). The people-oriented nature is the bright background of Xi Jinping Thought on the Rule of Law. *Beijing Daily*.

Cui, Y. (2021). The people-oriented nature of judicial system. *Oriental Law*, 5, 4–20. https://doi.org/10.19404/j.cnki.dffx.20210907.001

Deng, X. (1994). *1975—1982 Selected works of Deng Xiaoping (volume II)*. People's Publishing House.

Fu, Z., and Y. Zhang. 2021. People's standpoint and practical significance of Xi Jinping Thought on the Rule of Law. *Law Science* 6: 3–16.

Harold, J.B. 1974. *The interaction of law and religion.* Abingdon Press.

Hu, Y. (2021). Interpretation of the jurisprudence of "people-centeredness". *Oriental Law*, 2, 17–31. https://doi.org/10.19404/j.cnki.dffx.2021.02.002

Institute of Party History and Literature of CPC Central Committee. (2019). *The first volume of a selection of important documents since the 19th national congress of the Communist Party of China.* Central Party Literature Press.

Jean-Jacques, R. 1994. *Discourse on political economy and the social contract.* Oxford University Press.

Jin, D. 2022. Marxist concept of the people and the revolutionary logic of modern China. *Scientific Socialism* 1: 65–72.

Karl, M., & Frederick, E. (1976). *Collected works of Karl Marx and Frederick Engels.* Lawrence & Wishart Ltd.

Liu, H. (2021). Xi Jinping Thought on the Rule of Law and the construction of human rights protection system. *Chinese Journal of Human Rights*, 1, 1–12. https://doi.org/10.16133/j.cnki.xxlt.2021.05.018

Luo, S. 2021. Evaluation criteria and elements of the "good law and good governance" in China. *Tribune of Study* 5: 130–136.

Mao, Z. (1991). *Selected works Of Mao Zedong* (Volume III). People's Publishing House.

Mei, C. (2020, December 8). Adhering to the comprehensive promotion of impartial administration of justice. *Chongqing Daily.*

The Communist Party of China (CPC) Central Committee. (2020, December 8). Implementation outline for the construction of a society based on rule of law (2020–2025). *People's Daily.*

The Communist Party of China (CPC) Central Committee. (2021, August 12) . Implementation outline of the construction of government under the rule of law (2021—2025). *People's Daily.*

Party Documents Research Office of the CPC Central Committee. (2015). *Excerpt from Xi Jinping's speech on the comprehensive law-based governance.* Central Party Literature Press.

Qi, W. 2021. Xi Jinping Thought on socialism with Chinese characteristics for a new era and construction of Chinese-style modernization. *Jianghan Tribune* 9: 20–26.

Sun, Q. 2021. Inheritance and development of Marxist ideas of the rule of law by Xi Jinping Thought on the Rule of Law. *Chinese Journal of Law* 4: 3–20.

Tan, B., and Z. Liu. 2021. Theoretical support and guidance of Xi Jinping's Thought on the Rule of Law on social credit system. *Journal of Henan University of Economics and Law* 3: 7–16.

Tang, X. (2021, September 19). Accurately grasping the people-oriented nature of Xi Jinping Thought on the Rule of Law. *China Police Daily.*

The Communist Party of China (CPC) Central Committee. (2021, January 11). Construction plan of rule of law in China (2020—2025). *People's Daily.*

The Communist Party of China (CPC) Central Committee. (2021, January 11). Plan for the construction of China based on the rule of law (2020—2025). *People's Daily.*

Wang, X., Li, X., & Ma, Y. (2021, June 28). This country Is its people; the people are the country: general secretary Xi Jinping's important exposition on taking the people as the center. *People's Daily.*

Xi, J. 2021a. Unswervingly follow the path of socialist rule of law with Chinese characteristics to provide strong legal guarantee for the comprehensive construction of a modern socialist country. *Qiushi* 5: 4–15.

Xi, J. (2014). *Xi Jinping: the governance of China I.* Foreign Language Press.

Xi, J. (2016). *Speech at the meeting celebrating the 95th anniversary of the founding of the Communist Party of China.* Literature of Chinese Communist Party.

Xi, J. (2016, December 12). Implementation opinions on further integrating socialist core values into the construction of the rule of law. *People's Daily.*

Xi, J. (2017, October 28). Secure a decisive victory in building a moderately prosperous society in all respects and strive for the great success ofsocialism with Chinese characteristics for a new era. *People's Daily.*
Xi, J. (2018, May 5). Speech at the conference to commemorate the 200th anniversary of *Karl Marx*'s birth. *People's Daily.*
Xi, J. (2020). *On adhering to overall law-based governance of China.* Central Party Literature Press.
Xi, J. (2021, July 2). Speech at a ceremony marking the centenary of the Communist Party of China. *People's Daily.*
Xi, J. (2021, October 15). Uphold and improve the people's congress system and continuously enhancing whole-process people's democracy. *Guangming Daily.*
Xi, J. (2022, October 26). Hold high the great banner of socialism with Chinese characteristics and strive in unity to build a modern socialist country in all respects—report to the 20th national congress of the Communist Party of China. *People's Daily.*
Ying, Y. 2020. Discussion on the meeting, dilemma and the way Out of Xi Jinping's thought of national law-Abiding—a new dimension for examining the local ruling-by-law process. *Journal of Ningbo Open University* 1: 13–19.
Yu, F. 2021a. Commiting to a people-centered approach is the fundamental standpoint of Xi Jinping Thought on the Rule of Law. *Social Sciences in Chinese Higher Education* 1: 16–23.
Yu, Z. (2021). On the mission of rule of law in Xi Jinping Thought on the Rule of Law. *Journal of Shandong University(Philosophy and Social Sciences)*, 3, 10. https://doi.org/10.19836/j.cnki.37-1100/c.2021.03.002
Zhang, T. (2021, September 27). Unswervingly follow the path of socialist rule of law with Chinese characteristics—excerpt from the speech of the Forum on Xi Jinping Thought on the Rule of Law. *People's Daily.*
Zhang, W. (2021). The centenary course of the sinicization of Marxist jurisprudence. *Jilin University Journal Social Sciences Edition*, 4, 5–13. https://doi.org/10.15939/j.jujsse.2021.04.fx1
Zhou, S. (2021). Adhering to people-centered thought on the rule of law. *Law Science Magazine*, 1, 19–25. https://doi.org/10.16092/j.cnki.1001-618x.2021.01.003
Zhou, Y. (2021). The people's position and the fundamental viewpoints and methods of Xi Jinping Thought on the Rule of Law, (3) *Southeast Academic Research*, 3, 43–53. https://doi.org/10.13658/j.cnki.sar.2021.03.003

Chapter 7
Global Initiatives of Chinese Rule of Law Path

Abstract With Comrade *Xi Jinping* as the core, the Party Central Committee takes on the responsibility of a major country with the development concept of shared future. While creating a new path of Chinese rule of law modernization, it has also put forward a series of global governance principles to promote the transformation of the global governance system. The first is to respect the diversity of world cultures and promote the development of human rule of law civilization through exchanges and mutual learning. The second is to follow the principle of achieving shared growth through discussion and collaboration in engaging in global governance. The third is to promote the democracy, rule of law, and rationalization of international relations; The fourth is to adhere to the core values and fundamental principles of multilateralism and maintain the international system with the United Nations at its core and the international order based on international law; The fifth is to work to build a global community of shared future. The global governance principles of the contemporary Chinese Communists on the new path of Chinese rule of law modernization has been increasingly widely recognized and supported by the international community, which has effectively enhanced the discourse power and influence of the contemporary Chinese rule of law on the world rule of law stage.

7.1 Introduction

The world today is undergoing major changes unprecedented in a century. Global multipolarization, economic globalization, cultural diversification, and the development of information societies are all deepening trends. Countries are increasingly interconnected and interdependent. The rapid rise of emerging market countries and developing countries has made international forces more balanced, and peace and development have become the theme of the times. But at the same time, the world is faced with endless global challenges: regional conflicts continue, terrorism, cyber security, major infectious diseases, climate warming and other non-traditional security threats continue to spread, and the challenges facing mankind are increasingly complex and changeable. However, the current global governance system is more

© The Author(s), under exclusive license to Springer Nature Singapore Pte Ltd. 2024
X. Dong and J. Guo, *Chinese Rule of Law Path and Cultivation of Foreign-Related Rule of Law Talents*, https://doi.org/10.1007/978-981-97-2313-3_7

and more incompatible with the development situation and trend of the international community, and the international community is increasingly calling for the reform of the global governance system.

The Party Central Committee with Comrade *Xi Jinping* as its core, on the basis of respecting objective laws and grasping the general trend of development, has assumed the responsibility of a big country with the development concept of a common future in mind. In the process of creating the path of Chinese rule of law modernization, a series of global initiatives and practical measures to promote the transformation of the global governance system have been put forward.

First, we shall adhere to the global governance concept of joint discussion, building and sharing, abandon the old concept of cold war thinking and zero-sum game, adhere to mutual respect and understanding, enhance mutual learning and trust, resolve differences through consultation and dialogue, work together to address global challenges, build a better future for mankind, and let people of all countries enjoy development opportunities and achievements.

Second, we shall promote the democratization of international relations. Democracy is reflected in the people's ownership of the country within a country, and in the democratization of international relations between countries. The dignity of a country should be respected and its sovereignty, security and development interests should not be violated. It is anti-democratic to judge other countries by their own yardstick and even force them to copy their own political systems and democratic models through color revolution and the use of force.

Third, we shall practice true multilateralism, adhere to the core values and basic principles of multilateralism, maintain the international system with the United Nations at its core and the international order based on international law, promote the democratization, rule of law and rationalization of international relations, respect the sovereign equality of all countries, and promote the building of a global community of shared future based on rules, fairness and win–win results. At the practical level, China actively promotes the construction of a new type of international relations with win–win cooperation as the core, strives to build a peaceful and stable international development environment with an open and inclusive attitude, adheres to the opening strategy of "mutual benefit and win–win", strives to create a new platform for opening up, creates a comprehensive and diversified new pattern of opening up, and actively builds an open world economy.

Fourth, we shall build a global community of shared future. In order to promote the building of a global community of shared future, *Xi Jinping* announced a number of practical cooperation initiatives on a series of major international occasions, actively developed the global partnership, expanded the convergence of interests with countries, promoted cooperation, and adhered to the principle of joint consultation, joint construction and sharing, called on all knowledgeable people to work together to build the "the Belt and Road" development strategy, and promote the building of policy connectivity, facilities connectivity, smooth trade, financial integration The new platform for people to people cooperation not only provides a sustained impetus for economic growth for countries along the "the Belt and Road", but also contributes "China's wisdom" and "China's plan" to promoting the reform of the global governance system and addressing a shared future.

As more and more developing countries begin to have the right of speech in the global governance system, more and more Chinese initiatives are rising to international consensus, more and more Chinese initiatives are converging into international actions, more and more Chinese proposals are enlightening mankind in the direction of progress, and the global governance system is also increasingly developing in a more just and reasonable direction.

7.2 The Diversity and Interactivity of Rule of Law Civilization of Mankind

The diversity of civilization is the basic feature of the world and the source of human progress. The civilization of rule of law is an important part of human civilization, the core content of human political civilization, and also an important symbol of human civilization progress. It plays a role in safeguarding and promoting the entire human social civilization, including material as well as cultural and ethical civilization.

Firstly, the diversity of legal civilization is the inherent attribute of human civilization. The diversity of human civilization determines the diversity of human rule of law civilization. Since ancient times, China has formed a unique Chinese legal system in the history of the world's legal system and accumulated a profound legal culture. Unlike the civil law system, the common law system and the Islamic legal system, Chinese legal system was formed under the specific historical conditions of our country, showing the great creativity of the Chinese nation and the profound foundation of Chinese legal civilization. At the same time, Chinese legal system embodies the spirit and wisdom of the Chinese nation, and there are many excellent ideas and ideas worth our inheritance. The civilization of the rule of law in the western society originated from the political and legal practice of the ancient Greek city-state of Athens. Until the founding of the capitalist society in the seventeenth and eighteenth centuries, the legal world view with "rule of law" and "constitutionalism" as the core began to prevail. The proposed ideas such as "rule of law", "equality before the law", "judicial independence", "separation of powers", "freedom and equality", and "natural rights" have greatly enriched the Western Thought on the rule of law. The civilization of the rule of law realizes modernization in the collision and integration of China and the West.

The different breeding soil and unique historical process of human civilization have led to different paths and ways for human beings to pursue the civilization of the rule of law, thus forming different patterns of the rule of law. As *Xi Jinping* (2014: 16) stressed, there are no identical political systems in the world, neither is there a political model that fits all. The rule of law in modern Britain was gradually formed in the long-term struggle to limit the royal power, and gradually formed the British Constitution through the judicial practice of safeguarding human rights, which is manifested as a judicial-centered development model of the rule of law. The rule of law in France was deeply influenced by the revolution at the end of the eighteenth century and Rousseau's thought. It was manifested in the law-centered rule of law model, emphasizing that the parliament representing the people's sovereignty should formulate laws to protect human rights and freedoms. The rule of law model of the United States not only inherits the historical tradition of the common law system, but also is deeply influenced by the modern enlightenment thought of Europe. On the one hand, it is highlighted in the United States that civil liberties and rights should be protected by a written constitution, and the separation of powers should be established to achieve a balance between civil liberties and national rights; On the other hand, a constitutional review system has been established to highlight its role in the operation of the rule of law (Chen 2019: 20). The rule of law model in China is based on the achievements of the rule of law civilization that have been made in Chinese legal system, a socialist rule of law with Chinese characteristics developed in the continuous theoretical exploration and practical innovation of the CPC. It is precisely because of different human civilization systems and different national conditions that lead to the formation of different development paths of the rule of law, and thus the formation of various unique political systems and the rule of law system, and thus the whole human civilization is also mutually reinforcing and colorful.

Secondly, the interactivity of legal civilization is an important source of promoting the development of human civilization. The diverse development of human civilization has converged into the historical torrent of human civilization, and the progress of human civilization is to obtain a steady stream of powerful power from the diverse development of civilizations and exchanges among countries. Therefore, *Xi Jinping* (2020: 468) strongly advocated promoting exchanges and mutual learning among civilizations, pointing out that diversity spurs interaction among civilizations, which in turn promotes mutual learning and further development. The rule of law is one of the important achievements of human civilization, and the essence of the rule of law is of universal significance for national and social governance of all countries. We shall learn from the excellent achievements of the rule of law civilization in the world (Xi 2015a, b).

To begin with, human civilization is not isolated from each other. The diversity of human civilization determines the inherent inevitability of civilization exchange and mutual learning (Xi 2021: 65). With the rapid development of science and technology, the great improvement of communication methods, and the increasing advancement of economic globalization, the communication between human civilizations has gradually broken through the boundaries of time and space and broken the barriers of spirit and culture. The level, depth and breadth of communication have been greatly improved. The exchange and mutual learning of the rule of law civilization also makes the development process of human rule of law civilization full of vitality and vitality. It has been enriched by the introduction of Buddhism and the confluence of Islam and Confucianism in the old days, and by the introduction of Western learning, the launch of the New Culture Movement, and the introduction of Marxism and socialism in modern times. All-round opening up of the country, starting with the reform and opening-up program, has added to its vitality today (Xi 2020a, b: 471).

In addition, the multiple civilizations of mankind are equal, and we shall exchange and learn from each other on the basis of the principle of equality. All civilizations are rooted in their unique cultural environment. Each embodies the wisdom and vision of a country or nation, and each is valuable for being unique itself. Civilizations vary from each other only as human beings differ in terms of skin color and the language used. No civilization is superior to others It has its own value. Humans only have color and language differences, civilizations only have colorful differences, but there is no difference between high and low.... We need to be broad-minded and strive to remove all barriers to cultural exchanges. We need to be inclusive and always seek nourishment from other civilizations to promote the common development of Asian civilizations through exchanges and mutual learning. We should uphold equality and respect, abandon arrogance and prejudice, deepen our understanding of the differences between our own civilization and other civilizations, and promote the exchange of different civilizations Words and harmonious coexistence (Xi 2020a, b: 468). The history of the development of human civilization also proves that although there are differences in the history of various civilizations, there is no difference between the advantages and disadvantages of the highlands. All civilizations should be equal and respected equally. For the sustainable development of the civilization of the rule of law, we should treat all human civilizations equally, recognize the reality of long-term coexistence of different social systems and different cultures of the rule of law, adhere to the concept of diversified development, seek common ground while reserving differences, integrate each other in the collision, and learn from each other. This is not only in line with the objective reality of the diversity of human civilization, but also the internal law of the sustainable development of human civilization of the rule of law and is the only way to promote the continuous optimization of human civilization. Practice has proved that the socialist civilization of the rule of law with Chinese characteristics has unique advantages and strong vitality. To build a socialist country of rule of law, we must unswervingly follow the socialist road of rule of law with Chinese characteristics.

Last but not least, human civilization is inclusive, and we should promote the attitude of inclusiveness, seek common ground while reserving differences, and adhere to harmony but difference. We live on the same planet. It is home to more than 200 countries and regions, 2500-plus ethnic groups, and over 7 billion people. No attempt to erase their differences will work. Such differences are not a hindrance to exchanges, still less a cause for confrontation. Harmony in diversity and mutual learning between civilizations, social systems and paths can provide strong impetus for human progress. We should reject hubris and prejudice, treat each other with respect, stay open and inclusive, and embrace the diversity of our world. We should seek common ground while setting aside differences, draw upon each other's strengths, and pursue coexistence in harmony and win–win cooperation (Xi 2020a, b: 468). Chinese Thought on the diversity of world civilizations, on the one hand, affirms the diversity and difference, contradiction and conflict of human civilization, on the other hand, reaffirms the respect for the autonomy of all peoples in choosing their own development path and mode, opposes the hegemonic thought of "solipsism" in the process of civilization development, construction and innovation, and respects the independence and diversity of all human rule of law civilizations, overcomes prejudices and misunderstandings with an inclusive attitude, resists extremism and nationalism, and promotes global cooperation. Only by embracing each other and seeking common ground while reserving differences can human civilization develop in peace and harmony.

7.3 Adherence to the Global Governance Concept of Achieving Shared Growth Through Discussion and Collaboration

With the accelerated evolution of the world's international structure and the rise of the comprehensive strength of emerging market countries and developing countries, the global governance system inherited after the end of World War II is increasingly incompatible with the profound changes in international power; At the same time, new global governance issues continue to emerge, and human society is facing many challenges, such as climate warming, prevention and control of major infectious diseases, international governance in cyberspace, refugee crisis, and so on. At present, defects of the global governance system are increasingly apparent. The reform of the global governance system has become an inevitable trend. Since the 18th CPC National Congress, the Party Central Committee with Comrade *Xi Jinping* as its core has creatively put forward the global governance concept of discussion, joint development, and sharing of benefits on the basis of deeply grasping the trend of the world era and the development trend of human civilization, contributing Chinese wisdom to the reform of the global governance system and solving the problems of world governance.

The concept of global governance based on discussion, collaboration and sharing is the basic concept and initiative of China's active participation in the reform and construction of the global governance system. It follows the independent diplomatic position of previous CPC members, inherits and develops China's foreign policy of peace, adheres to the diplomatic concept of friendly consultation, seeking common ground while reserving differences, and stands on a historical height to grasp the global trend, the concept of governance based on the people.

1. Discussion is the Foundation of Global Governance

Discussion refers to the democratization of global governance. In the report to the 19th CPC National Congress, President *Xi Jinping* (2017) pointed out that China follows the principle of achieving shared growth through discussion and collaboration in engaging in global governance. China stands for democracy in international relations and the equality of all countries, big or small, strong or weak, rich or poor. In other words, countries, big or small, strong or weak, enjoy equal opportunities, equal rights and equal rules. Communication and mutual understanding on the basis of equality are the basis of achieving global governance. The so-called equality of opportunity means that in all areas of global governance, in the face of common problems and challenges of mankind, every sovereign country is an equal member of the international community, and has equal opportunities to participate in decision-making, to express their appeals and positions, and to enjoy the governance results. The equality of rights means that every sovereign country in the international community enjoys the rights conferred by international law and undertakes the obligations conferred by the international community on sovereign countries. Rule equality means opposing hegemonism, nationalism, pragmatism and double standards in the face of international rules. All sovereign countries should be required to abide by international rules without discrimination.

Discussion is recognizing differences and seeking consensus. More than 200 countries and regions around the world have varying degrees of differences in their historical backgrounds, economic development levels, legal systems, religious beliefs, cultural traditions, and many other aspects, which inevitably lead to conflicts of civilizations and differences in interests. However, global challenges and governance challenges have global characteristics because they are not just difficulties faced by a particular country or region. At the same time, it also goes beyond the governance scope and capacity of a single sovereign state, requiring countries to work together and govern together. President *Xi Jinping* (2017) has repeatedly emphasized that all countries are entitled to shape the future of the world, making international rules, managing global affairs and sharing the fruits of development. Therefore, only through mutual consultation and seeking common ground while reserving differences on the basis of respecting differences can we expand cooperation space, reach political consensus on global governance, economic development consensus, and social development consensus, and ultimately achieve the goal of win–win cooperation.

2. Collaboration is the Path of Global Governance

Collaboration is the fundamental path for countries to achieve global governance based on discussion and consensus. Collaboration means that all countries should participate in global construction, jointly promote cooperation, jointly assume obligations in the process of global governance, jointly solve global governance problems, achieve common development, and share common achievements. One aspect of collaboration is to jointly address global challenges. In today's globalized world, the entire world is a universally connected organic whole, forming a close-knit community of shared development. Countries share weal and woe, constrain and interact with each other. In the face of global governance challenges and governance dilemmas, no country can stand alone, and many challenges are difficult to independently address, which requires all countries to adhere to the concept of collaboration, work together, give full play to the strengths and potential, do best to achieve mutual benefits, and achieve win–win results. However, it should also be noted that developing countries still have differences in their capabilities and development levels compared with developed countries, and they should bear common but differentiated responsibilities under the same goal. Another aspect of collaboration is to achieve changes in the global governance system. Today's world is in the midst of great changes that have not been seen in a century. The international architecture is evolving rapidly, the trend of world multi-polarization and economic globalization has deepened, and the global governance system and multilateral cooperation mechanisms are challenged by protectionism and unilateralism. In order to promote the construction of a peaceful, developmental, cooperative, and win–win international community, the global governance mechanism urgently needs to be reformed.

The concept of collaboration proposed by President *Xi Jinping* is to advocate for countries to jointly establish an international system with the United Nations as the core and an international order based on international law. In the current situation, the role of the United Nations needs to be strengthened, not weakened. To jointly build a new international order with the United Nations at its core is to promote innovation and improvement in the global governance system, promote equal rights, rules, and opportunities, enhance the representation and voice of emerging market and developing countries, and ensure the equal participation of all countries in rule-making, while maintaining the international status of the United Nations, striving for more equal and fair development opportunities.

3. Sharing is the Goal of Global Governance

Collaboration is the basis of sharing, and the goal of collaboration is sharing. The primary connotation of sharing is that all sovereign countries share the development achievements of the world in economic, cultural, ecological and other global governance through coordinated governance. *Xi Jinping* (2015) stressed that all countries should become participants, contributors and beneficiaries of global development. One country could not develop without the development of other countries, and some countries could not develop without the development of other countries. That is to say, the results of global governance should be shared fairly and justly by the participants in the joint construction to achieve win–win cooperation and common development, which is the core of *Xi Jinping*'s concept of collaboration and sharing. *Xi Jinping*'s concept of sharing is not only the driving force to attract countries to actively participate in joint discussion and construction, but also an important guarantee to promote the concept of joint discussion and construction of governance. Only by fully ensuring that all countries enjoy equal rights, equal opportunities, and equal rules to share the construction results of global governance, can the cornerstone of trust between countries become more stable, the team of joint construction become stronger, the trend of globalization become more stable, and global development become more balanced, The construction achievements will also benefit the people of all countries more and more equitably, so that human development can prosper.

The concept of achieving shared growth through discussion and collaboration is a development concept timely put forward in response to the new situation at home and abroad in the new era, and a governance concept adapted to the reform of global governance mechanism. The concept of shared growth reflects the urgent desire and development needs of emerging market countries and developing countries to break the pattern of western countries occupying the monopoly privilege of world governance and actively participate in the process of global governance. It is an effective means to balance the dispute between developing countries and developed countries over the right to speak, and a good way to promote the development of the world towards fairness and justice. As the largest developing country, China has actively promoted the reform of the global governance system while promoting national governance and national construction. It has always adhered to the global governance concept of achieving shared growth through discussion and collaboration, adhered to the opening strategy of mutual benefit and win–win results, worked hard to create a friendly and stable international environment, actively built a global partnership, gathered consensus, promote international cooperation through the Belt and Road Initiative. In doing so, we hope to achieve policy, infrastructure, trade, financial, and people-to-people connectivity and thus build a new platform for international cooperation to create new drivers of shared development.

4. Values of the Global Governance Concept

The global governance concept of achieving shared growth through discussion and collaboration is the Chinese wisdom contributed by China's active participation in the transformation and construction of the global governance system. It is a Chinese solution provided to solve the governance challenges faced by the world, and also an important component of Chinese Thought on socialist ideology with Chinese characteristics in the new era, with profound theoretical and rich practical values.

(1) Theoretical Values

Firstly, at the beginning of the founding of the People's Republic of China, the leaders of the Party Central Committee, represented by *Mao Zedong* and *Deng Xiaoping*, proposed to always adhere to an independent foreign policy of peace based on a profound examination of the domestic and international situation. No matter how difficult and complex the external environment may be, we must ensure that China handles domestic and foreign affairs in an independent and manner and is not subject to imperialist intervention and oppression. On the basis of practicing this diplomatic concept, Premier *Zhou Enlai* creatively proposed the Five Principles of Peaceful Coexistence at the Bandung Conference, which was widely recognized by various countries and has become one of the important principles of international communication. After the reform and opening up, facing the complex international situation, *Deng Xiaoping* further proposed the development concept of seeking common ground while reserving differences on the basis of foreign policy of peace, proposing to put aside disputes for joint development. In today's turbulent world situation, President *Xi Jinping*, on the basis of inheriting China's foreign policy of peace, has always adhered to the diversity of world civilization, respected the diversity of the world, adhered to the development concept of seeking common ground while reserving differences, and further proposed the global governance concept of achieving shared growth through discussion and collaboration with a great mind of inclusiveness. The global governance concept of achieving shared growth through discussion and collaboration not only inherits and develops the wise diplomatic ideas of previous

CPC members, enriches the theory of major country diplomacy with Chinese characteristics, but also conforms to the trend of the times and the theme of development, bringing impetus and opportunities to the reform of the world governance system.

Secondly, the global governance concept of of achieving shared growth through discussion and collaboration enrich Chinese Thought on socialist ideology with Chinese characteristics in the new era. The challenges in today's world are continuous, and mankind is in an era of increasing risks. The world economic growth is sluggish, the impact of the financial crisis lingers on, and the development gap is widening. Armed conflicts occur from time to time. Cold War mentality and power politics still exist. Non-conventional security threats, particularly terrorism, refugee crises, major communicable diseases and climate change, are spreading. The international order is damaged, and the global governance system and multilateral mechanisms have been impacted. The global governance concept of achieving shared growth through discussion and collaboration not only inherits and develops the wise diplomatic ideas of previous CPC members, enriches the theory of major country diplomacy with Chinese characteristics, but also conforms to the trend of the times and the theme of development, bringing impetus and opportunities to the reform of the world governance system. The CPC, with Comrade *Xi Jinping* as its core, has followed the trend of the times, responded to the call of the times, and proposed a global governance concept of achieving shared growth through discussion and collaboration, injecting vitality into promoting the democracy, rule of law, and rationalization of global governance, and promoting world peace and development. This is the governance of China's participation in global governance, reflecting the Chinese style, Chinese characteristics, and Chinese wisdom. It is an innovation and development of the socialist ideology with Chinese characteristics in the new era, a wise thinking and unique insights on major issues of human development, expanding the path for developing countries to modernization, and providing choices and opportunities for countries and nations seeking development while maintaining their independence.

(2) Practical Values

Firstly, the global governance concept of achieving shared growth through discussion and collaboration have promoted the transformation of the global governance system. With the rapid rise of emerging market countries and the rise of the comprehensive strength of developing countries, power structures among various countries are changing positively in an unprecedented way. The trend of rising in the east and falling in the west and rising in the south and falling in the north has become more obvious. The original global governance system led by developed countries can no longer cope with the changes of the new world order. The trend of hegemonism and unilateralism has seriously hindered the progress and development of the world. The governance mechanism and discourse power structure urgently need to be updated and improved. The global governance concept of achieving shared growth through discussion and collaboration is precisely a prescription for treating the symptoms of global governance, supplementing and improving the existing world governance pattern and global governance theory, pointing out the development direction for global governance system reform, and provides institutional guarantee.

Secondly, the global governance concept of achieving shared growth through discussion and collaboration has promoted the Belt and Road Initiative. In order to deepen reform and strive to build a new pattern of win–win cooperation in opening up, Comrade *Xi Jinping* put forward the Belt and Road Initiative in 2013, which has built a new platform for connectivity and international cooperation for world development and added new impetus to common development. President *Xi Jinping* (2017) pointed out that the Belt and Road Initiative was launched in response to the call for reforming the global governance system. The Belt and Road Initiative promotes partnership and a community of shared future, shared rights and joint responsibilities. It offers a new approach to reform and improvement of the global governance system. The Belt and Road Initiative aims to enhance connectivity and results-oriented cooperation. It is about working together to meet the challenges and risks that confront humanity, and delivering win–win outcomes and common development. The proposal of the global governance concept of achieving shared growth through discussion and collaboration has provided fundamental compliance and important policy guarantees for the specific implementation of the Belt and Road Initiative. To promote the Belt and Road Initiative, we need to adhere to equality-based dialogue and friendly consultations, resolve differences, plan for overall development, and build the Belt and Road into the broadest international cooperation platform conforming to the trend of economic globalization through bilateral cooperation, trilateral cooperation, multilateral cooperation and other forms, so as to allow more countries to participate, give play to the advantages of linkage, promote the integration of the world economy, achieve common development for all mankind and realize the great vision of a global community of shared future.

7.4 Promotion of Democracy, Rule of Law and Rationalization of International Relations

The world today is in the historical process of restructuring the global governance system. Global governance is facing many serious global challenges, such as governance deficit, trust deficit, peace deficit, development deficit, and so on. General Secretary *Xi Jinping* has a profound insight into the historical orientation and trend of the great changes in the world today that have not occurred in a century and upholds the concept of building a global community of shared future, and puts forward the idea of jointly promoting the democracy, rule of law and rationalization of international relations, which provides a Chinese plan for promoting the reform of the global governance system.

The first is to jointly promote the democracy of international relations. The basic spirit of the democracy of international relations is to oppose power politics and unilateralism, and all countries in the world should solve international problems and jointly govern international affairs through equal consultation. In international affairs, we must adhere to the five principles of peaceful coexistence and abandon the jungle rule of the jungle of the jungle of the jungle of the jungle. Countries, regardless of size, wealth, and strength, are equal members of the international community. They are equal not only in rights and interests, but also in international rules, and have the right to participate in regional and international affairs on an equal basis. Democratization of international relations is the voice of the times and the key and prerequisite for building a harmonious world and promoting lasting peace, common development and progress of civilization. Without the democratization of international relations, multi-polarization and globalization will go astray, a just and reasonable new international order would not be established, and the lofty goal of world peace and development will be difficult to achieve.

After experiencing the epidemic, people of all countries have come to a clearer understanding of the need to abandon Cold War mentality and zero-sum games, oppose any form of "new Cold War" and ideological confrontation, and treat each other equally and with mutual respect. Sovereignty is the fundamental symbol of national independence, as well as the fundamental manifestation and reliable guarantee of national interests. Sovereign equality has been the most important criterion for regulating relations between countries for hundreds of years, and it is also the primary principle followed by the United Nations and all agencies and organizations. To uphold fairness and justice in international relations and global governance, we must first uphold the principle of national sovereignty and equality, which is the most important criterion in international relations and the primary principle that global governance must follow.

The second is to jointly promote the rule of law in international relations. The establishment of a just and reasonable international order is the goal and ideal of mankind. In the era of globalization, the boundaries between the domestic and international levels tend to be blurred, the mutual connection and penetration are strengthened, and the mutual influence and transformation are accelerated. The value orientation and political wisdom of domestic and international governance are highly unified, and the international and domestic rules with law as the main content are also interlinked in essence. As an external manifestation and logical extension of the concept and basic strategy of overall law-based governance, *Xi Jinping* (2019: 171) advocated the rule of law and the maintenance of international fairness and justice in global governance, which also conforms to the trend of the rule of law in international relations. The establishment of international mechanisms, the observance of international rules and the pursuit of international justice have become the consensus of most countries. It is necessary to improve the status and role of international law in global governance and ensure the effective observance and implementation of international rules. It is the responsibility of all countries to safeguard the authority of the international rule of law, adhere to the equal importance of rights and obligations, exercise rights in accordance with the law, and perform obligations in good faith. To promote the reform of the global governance system, it is necessary to ensure the equal and uniform application of international law, and oppose distortion International law opposes any act that infringes on the legitimate rights and interests of other countries and undermines international peace and stability in the name of the rule of law. The rule of law is the rule of rules. With the deepening of global governance reform, it is imperative to constantly improve the international rule system and ensure the fairness and justice of the international order and human society. Therefore, we must adhere to the rule orientation and improve global governance.

The last is to jointly promote the rationalization of international relations. Countries are closely linked, and mankind shares a common destiny. President *Xi Jinping* (2019: 169) pointed out that we should promote the construction of a new type of international relations featuring mutual respect, fairness and justice, and win–win cooperation. The goal of the reform of the global governance system is to make global governance develop in a direction that more balanced reflects the wishes and interests of most countries, especially emerging market countries and developing countries, so as to better reflect the changes in the international pattern, meet the practical needs of addressing global challenges, and comply with the historical trend of peaceful development and win–win cooperation. It is normal for countries to have differences. It should be properly resolved through dialogue and consultation. There can be competition among countries, but it must be positive and benign, and we must keep the moral bottom line and international norms. A big country should look like a big country. It should provide more global public goods, assume its responsibilities and show its responsibility. China has actively participated in the reform and construction of the global governance system and promoted the reform of unfair and unreasonable arrangements in the global governance system. Efforts should be made to make the global governance system more balanced in reflecting the wishes and interests of most countries, especially emerging market countries and developing countries, in order to better reflect changes in the international landscape, meet the practical needs of addressing global challenges, and comply with the historical trend of peaceful development and win–win cooperation. It is normal for countries to have differences. It should be resolved through dialogue and negotiation. There can be competition between countries, but it must be positive and benign, and we must uphold the moral bottom line and international norms. A major country should have the appearance of a major country, provide more global public goods, bear the responsibility of a major country, and demonstrate the responsibility of a major country.

China actively participates in the reform and construction of the global governance system and promotes the transformation of unfair and unreasonable arrangements in the global governance system, striving to make the global governance system more balanced in reflecting the will and interests of most countries. As a participant, promoter, and leader in the process of global governance change, China plays a constructive role by actively participating in and striving to lead international rule-making, promoting the formation of a fair, reasonable, and transparent international rule system, firmly safeguarding the common interests of developing countries, enhancing the status and role of developing countries in the global governance system, and enhancing China's voice and influence in the global governance system change, striving to contribute Chinese wisdom and solutions to improving the global governance system.

7.5 Practice of True Multilateralism

Multilateralism is an effective path to maintain peace and promote development. Its essence is that international affairs are jointly discussed and handled by everyone, and the future and destiny of the world are jointly controlled by all countries. For a long time, China has held high the banner of multilateralism, actively participated in multilateral activities centered around the United Nations, and extensively participated in multilateral treaties and international conventions, making great contributions to maintaining world peace and promoting common development. Although peace and development remain the themes of the times, the world still faces many problems and challenges. Unilateralism and protectionism are still prevalent in some countries, which continue to affect the stability and development of the international community; The world economy is facing the most severe recession since World War II; Cultural soft power such as ideology, values, and moral norms are increasingly becoming the main battlefield of competition between countries; Global issues such as climate change, environmental pollution, and major infectious diseases continue to threaten the survival homeland of all humanity... These issues are intertwined and fermenting, forming common difficulties and challenges on the path of human progress. At the same time, the trend of multi-polarity in the world has not fundamentally changed, and economic globalization has shown new resilience. The call to uphold multilateralism and strengthen communication and cooperation has become even stronger.

Firstly, to practice true multilateralism, it is necessary to uphold the concept of a global community of shared future, uphold the common values of peace, development, fairness, justice, democracy, and freedom for all mankind, break free from ideological biases, maximize the openness and inclusiveness of cooperation mechanisms, concepts, and policies, and jointly maintain world peace and stability. A peaceful and developing world should carry different forms of civilization and must be compatible with various paths towards modernization. We must vigorously promote the common values of all humanity, compete on the basis of fairness and justice, build an open world economy, firmly uphold the multilateral trading system, do not engage in discriminatory and exclusive standards, rules, and systems, do not create high barriers that separate trade, investment, and technology, and engage in track and field competitions that catch up with each other and improve together, rather than engaging in fierce competition. Some developed countries often exhibit a self-interest tendency in the construction and operation of relevant multilateral mechanisms. This "selective multilateralism" follows the logic of prioritizing national interests, which is inconsistent with the realization of the common interests of humanity and hinders the deepening of multilateral cooperation and the unity of the international community. China advocates upholding the concept of a community with a shared future for mankind and making promoting common development among all countries and addressing global development imbalances an important agenda for international multilateral cooperation. In the established multilateral system, countries should act in accordance with corresponding rules and procedures, maintain the authority and effectiveness of the multilateral system, and cannot choose according to their own will in fulfilling obligations and complying with rules. International rules should be jointly observed by all countries, and there should be no exceptions. The multilateral system should also be continuously innovated and improved in practice to better coordinate the actions of countries and respond to challenges, but it cannot be used as a tool for cooperation or for abandonment if not in accordance.

Secondly, to practice true multilateralism, we must adhere to international law as the foundation and effectively maintain a fair and just system, order, and rules. An ancient Chinese philosopher said, "law is the very foundation of governance." The international community should govern according to the rules and consensus reached by all countries, rather than being dictated by one or several countries. There is only one system in the world, which is the international system with the United Nations at its core. There is only one order, which is based on international law. There is only one set of rules, which is the fundamental norms of international relations based on the purposes and principles of the United Nations Charter. The United Nations has developed into the most universal, representative, and authoritative international organization in the world today. It is a symbol of multilateralism and the core of multilateral mechanisms. The Charter of the United Nations is recognized as the basic norms of state to state relations. Without these universally recognized international norms jointly formulated by the international community, the world will eventually slide into the law of the jungle of the jungle, which will bring disastrous consequences to mankind. To solve international affairs, we cannot start from the so-called "power status" and promote hegemony and bullying. The practice of the strong bullying the weak is not multilateralism. China adheres to the international rule of law and unwaveringly upholds the international system with the United Nations at its core, the international order based on international law, and the basic norms of international relations based on the purposes and principles of the United Nations Charter. Multilateral institutions are the platform for practicing multilateralism and the basic framework for maintaining it, and their authority and effectiveness should be upheld. The multilateral mechanism with the United Nations at its core not only represents the progress of the international community, but also marks a new era where "all countries, big or small, being equal" is no longer an empty phrase.

Thirdly, to practice true multilateralism, we should oppose "pseudo multilateralism". On the surface, pseudo multilateralism carries the banner of multilateralism, but in essence, it involves engaging in "exclusive groups" and group politics, and even using ideology to stand in line and choose sides between camps to divide the world, disrupt international order, create confrontation and division. Some Western countries view the multilateral system as a tool for individual countries or a few countries to consolidate or expand their dominant position in the world, often excluding the majority of countries with ideological lines. Imposing one's own values, norms, rules, etc. on other countries through a multilateral system seriously undermines their sovereign equality and voice in world affairs. Multilateralism should not be closed and exclusive. Multilateralism in a small circle deviates from the original intention and essence of multilateralism and is a "pseudo multilateralism" that practices unilateralism in the name of multilateralism. We must adhere to openness and inclusiveness, and not engage in closed exclusivity. The essence of multilateralism is that international affairs are handled by everyone through consultation, and the future and destiny of the world are jointly controlled by all countries. Engaging in "exclusive groups" or "new Cold War" internationally, excluding, threatening, intimidating others, and easily engaging in decoupling, supply cutting, and sanctions, artificially causing mutual isolation or even isolation, can only push the world towards division or even confrontation. A divided world cannot cope with the common challenges facing humanity, and confrontation will lead humanity to a dead end. We firmly oppose the practice of the strong bullying the weak, reversing black and white, and practicing unilateralism in the name of multilateralism; We firmly oppose using international rules as a tool to maintain our own hegemony, using our own interests as the standard, and engaging in "selective multilateralism". The world should be fair, not domineering. At present, the century long changes in the world and the century long pandemic are intertwined and overlapping, and the international landscape is accelerating its evolution. The turbulent adjustment is still ongoing. In the complex international situation, multilateralism faces many challenges. True multilateralism goes hand in hand with the democratization and rule of law in international relations, advocating for the equality of large and small countries, and handling state to state relations through cooperation, negotiation, and consultation rather than power, force, or coercion. Engaging in group politics, small circles, and other "pseudo multilateralism" runs counter to true multilateralism and is incompatible with the trend of the times and the expectations of the people.

Fourth, practicing true multilateralism requires the joint support and maintenance of members of the international community, as well as the contribution and demonstration of major powers. Multilateralism in modern international relations originates from human efforts to solve common problems. In an increasingly interconnected world, no country, no matter how powerful, can stand alone and solve the problems facing the world on its own. Instead, it needs to attach importance to multilateral cooperation and the multilateral system from a strategic and principled perspective. Multilateralism is not a tree without roots, but a product that adapts to the requirements of the era of economic globalization and world multi-polarity. To revive multilateralism, major countries in the world should become role models in adhering to the purposes and principles of the United Nations Charter, leaders in following international rules, and pioneers in providing necessary international public goods for global well-being. It is particularly important that major powers in the world lead the international community to firmly establish the concept of a global community of shared future, raise the banner of openness, inclusiveness, cooperation, and win–win results, uphold the common values of peace, development, fairness, justice, democracy, and freedom for all mankind, and further deepen and expand the connotation and extension of multilateralism. President *Xi Jinping* (2020b) pointed out that in the twenty-first century, multilateralism should adhere to the core values and fundamental principles of multilateralism and face the future. It should also be based on changes in the world landscape, focus on addressing global challenges, and reform and improve the global governance system on the basis of extensive consultation and consensus building. Maintaining and practicing true multilateralism is an inevitable choice for humanity to respond to global challenges and solve global problems and is of great significance for human peace and development. China firmly adheres to the core values and basic principles of multilateralism, based on changes in the world pattern, focuses on addressing global challenges, and continuously enriches the practice of multilateralism in the new situation. Standing on the right side of history and on the side of human progress, China has continuously written new chapters on safeguarding and practicing multilateralism.

7.6 Working to Build a Global Community of Shared Future

In the report of the 19th National Congress of the CPC, President *Xi Jinping*(2017) made a clear statement: We call on the people of all countries to work together to build a community with a shared future for mankind, to build an open, inclusive, clean, and beautiful world that enjoys lasting peace, universal security, and common prosperity. On December 1, 2017, in the speech at the high-level dialogue between the CPC and the world political parties, General Secretary *Xi Jinping* (2018: 510) clearly expressed the basic meaning of a global community of shared future, as the term suggests, a global community of shared future means that the future of each and every nation and country is interlocked. We are in the same boat, and we should stick together, share weal and woe, endeavor to build this planet of ours into a single harmonious family, and turn people's longing for a better life into reality. Therefore, it is the ardent expectation of the people of all countries in the world to grasp the general trend of world development, follow the trend of the times, promote the development of the international order and international system in a more just and reasonable direction, promote the building of a global community of shared future, let the torch of peace pass from generation to generation, let the power of development continue, and let the light of civilization shine.

Working to build a global community of shared future is a significant strategic idea with rich connotations and profound implications, reflecting the objective laws of human social development. In the long history of human social development, the contradictory movement between productive forces and forms of communication has formed a sequence of organic connections. The process of transforming history from early modern times to world history is rooted in the historical progress of social productivity and the resulting changes in production methods. Since entering the modern world, the scope of activities that influence each other among different ethnic groups has been expanding day by day. The isolated and free survival state of ethnic groups in the past has gradually been broken and incorporated into a holistic and interconnected development network. As a result, isolated or divided history began to shift towards a holistic or unified history, which gave birth to the emergence of modern international law and the establishment and development of the international system. President *Xi Jinping* (2018: 415) insisted on applying the basic principles of Marxism historical materialism and the theory of world history to thoroughly investigate the evolution process of political civilization and international order of human society since modern times, summarized the human social history of the last 100 years, and drew an important conclusion: peace and development are the common aspirations of all mankind, and as modern history shows, to establish a fair and equitable international order is the goal for which humanity has always striven. However, this task has not yet been completed. Therefore, we must comply with the trend of history and the voice of the people, work to build a global community of shared future, and make unremitting efforts to achieve the noble goal of world peace and development, and establish a more just and reasonable international order and global governance system.

The major strategic idea of working to build a global community of shared future crystallizes the common values of humanity. Civilization is the soul of a country or a nation. The civilization of every country and nation is deeply rooted in the social soil of their own country and nation. However, there are undoubtedly certain common value factors between each civilization system under different time and space conditions. With the enhancement and expansion of human social interaction, the common value factors hidden behind different civilization systems are bound to emerge in various ways and means. These common value factors undoubtedly reflect the rational requirements of the universality of human social interaction practice. President *Xi Jinping* (2018: 5) stands at a new historical starting point in promoting the construction of a community with a shared future for mankind, refining and summarizing the common values of human society accumulated in the process of human civilization development, and elaborating insightfully on the common values of human society, profoundly pointing out that peace, development, fairness, justice, democracy, and freedom are the common values of all humanity. Based on the common values of humanity—peace, development, equity, justice, democracy and freedom—China is committed to advocating exchanges and mutual learning among civilizations, so as to promote the development of human civilization. This important idea reflects the unremitting pursuit of the development and progress of human civilization, reflects the common value concern of all humanity, and highlights the noble humanistic sentiment that a just cause should be pursued for the common good, thus establishing the common human values that build a global community of shared future. Furthermore, it fully demonstrates China's wisdom in responding to the world question.

The new concept of working to build a global community of shared future embodies the outstanding achievements of Chinese civilization and the common value pursuit of all mankind and reflects the historic changes in relationship between China and the World in the new era. Once it was put forward, it has generated strong resonance around the world. It has been included in the declarations and outcome documents of various United Nations agreements and international multilateral mechanisms, and has triggered positive responses at the national level, regional level and major global fields. It has gained more and more recognition and support from the international community and has demonstrated its strong international influence. It is moving forward from concept to action and towards building a global community of shared future. As President *Xi Jinping* (2020a: 276) pointed out, since the 18th National Congress of the Communist Party of China, we have proposed the concept of promoting the construction of a global community of shared future, which has been widely welcomed and highly praised by all parties and has been included in a series of resolutions of the United Nations. We must seize the opportunity and take advantage of the situation, firmly uphold the international order and system centered on the United Nations Charter and principles and contribute Chinese wisdom and solutions to the reform and construction of the global governance system.

7.7 Conclusion

The era process of the contemporary CPC to expand the new path of Chinese rule of law modernization is intrinsically intertwined with the great changes in the world's rule of law civilization, which historically reshapes the development pattern of the world's rule of law civilization and contains the basic value elements of the new form of human rule of law civilization. Civilized diversity is the basic feature of human society and the inexhaustible driving force of human progress. The diversity of civilizations determines the inherent inevitability of exchanges and mutual learning among civilizations. The development of human civilization under the rule of law is not only one model, and different civilizations under the rule of law are the crystallization of human governance wisdom. China advocates the concept of equality, mutual learning, dialogue and inclusiveness, and advocates that different civilizations under the rule of law can fully exchange and learn from each other. While exploring its own path of the rule of law, China also provides a platform for exchanges and mutual learning among different legal civilizations.

Every civilization is unique, and all achievements of civilization are worthy of respect and treasure. There is no clash of civilizations. Although each civilization system is in different time and space conditions, there are undoubtedly some similar value factors. Standing at a new historical starting point in promoting the building of a global community of shared future, President *Xi Jinping* (2018: 253) articulated the common values of all humanity, emphasizing the need to promote the common values of all humanity, including peace, development, fairness, justice, democracy, and freedom to promote mutual understanding and forge closer bonds with other peoples, and to respect the diversity of civilizations. This important idea not only leads the progress of human political civilization development, but also highlights the beautiful future of human social development. Faced with the "world question" that what has happened to the world and how should we respond, President *Xi Jinping* creatively proposed a major strategic idea to build a global community of shared future, emphasizing the need to adhere to dialogue and consultation, build a world of lasting peace, promote fair and just global governance, and jointly promote the democracy of international relations. We should adhere to true multilateralism and push global order and governance to develop in a fairer and more reasonable way. We should follow the principle of achieving shared growth through discussion and collaboration, build a universally safe world, and jointly promote the rule of law in international relations. All countries must adhere to universally recognized international laws, adhere to internationally agreed upon agreements. The concept of a global community of shared future reveals the objective law that all countries in the world are interdependent and the destiny of mankind is closely linked, reflects the common values of all humanity, and finds the "greatest common denominator" for building a better world together. The proposal and practice of major strategic ideas to build a global community of shared future deeply reflect the historic changes in China's relations with the world in the new era and have formed a strong international influence. The core essence of multilateralism is that international affairs are jointly discussed and handled by everyone, and the future and destiny of the world are jointly controlled by all countries. Countries should respect each other's sovereignty and core interests, abandon ideological biases, cultivate and enhance mutual trust, bridge differences through dialogue, and solve problems through consultation. To promote the building of a global community of shared future on the basis of multilateralism, we need to promote civilized exchanges that are harmonious but diverse and inclusive. We should replace the "clash of civilizations" and "superiority of civilizations" with a new concept of civilization that is colorful, equal, and inclusive, and promote mutual learning and harmonious coexistence among different civilizations. To promote the building of a global community of shared future on the basis of multilateralism, it is necessary to build an ecological civilization system that respects nature and green development. All countries should work together to fulfill their responsibilities and forge a new path of green, low-carbon, circular and sustainable development.

Looking forward to the future, China will always stand on the right side of history, always be a loyal builder of world peace, an active contributor to global development, a common defender of the international order and a strong supporter of multilateralism, and make new and greater contributions to building a world of lasting peace, universal security, common prosperity, openness, inclusiveness, and clean and beautiful. It is obvious that the global initiatives of the contemporary CPC on the new path of Chinese rule of law modernization is increasingly widely recognized and supported by the international community, which has effectively promoted the contemporary Chinese rule of law in the world rule of law arena.

References

Chen, H. (2019). The exploration and contribution of Chinese path to the rule of law civilization. *Southeast Academic Research*, 6, 20–28. https://doi.org/10.13658/j.cnki.sar.2019.06.003

Compilation Group of Introduction to Xi Jinping Thought on the Rule of Law. (2021). I*ntroduction to Xi Jinping Thought on the Rule of Law*. Higher Education Press.

The Publicity Department of the CPC Central Committee. 2019. *Introduction to Xi Jinping Thought on the socialism with Chinese characteristics for the new era*. People's Publishing House.

Xi, J. 2014. *Speech at the celebration of the 60th anniversary of the founding of the national people's congress*. People's Publishing House.

Xi, J. 2015. Promote socialist rule of law. *Qiushi*, 1.

Xi, J. 2015. Seeking common and sustainable development and becoming a win-win partner in cooperation—speech at the United Nations Development Summit. *People's Daily*, September 27.
Xi, J. 2017. *Xi Jinping: The governance of China II*. Foreign Language Press.
Xi, J. 2017. Secure a decisive victory in building a moderately prosperous society in all respects and strive for the great success of socialism with Chinese characteristics for a new era. *People's Daily*, October 28.
Xi, J. 2018. *On building a global community of shared future*. Central Party Literature Press.
Xi, J. 2020a. *On adhering to overall law-based governance of China*. Central Party Literature Press.
Xi, J. 2020b. *Xi Jinping: the governance of China III*. Foreign Language Press.

Chapter 8
Cultivation of Foreign-Related Rule of Law Talents

Abstract Strengthening the construction of foreign-related rule of law, participating in global governance, and striving for discourse power in international rule of law call for the cultivation of a large number of foreign-related rule-of-law professional talents. The construction of foreign-related rule of law is an important connotation of Chinese Thought on the Rule of Law, which provides the direction and defines specific tasks and requirements for the cultivation of foreign-related rule-of-law professional talents in the new era. Since the reform and opening up, China has made some achievements in the cultivation of foreign-related rule-of-law talents, but there are also multiple problems, such as the lack of top-level design, the insufficient overall number of talents, imperfect education system, insufficient language capacity and so on. Guided by Chinese Thought on the Rule of Law and driven by the problem-oriented path, this chapter presents a theoretical framework of national foreign-related rule-of-law language capacity covering "five kinds of competence"—governance, monitoring, standardization, education as well as intelligence, and puts forward some suggestions for the cultivation of foreign-related rule-of-law talents, aiming to provide some references for colleges and universities to deeply implement Chinese Thought on the Rule of Law.

8.1 Introduction

The concept of "national language capacity" stems from western academic circles. At the end of the twentieth century, Richard and Ronald (1993: 532), scholars at the advanced language research center of the University of Maryland, put forward the concept of national language capacity from the perspectives of national security, national needs and the ability to meet needs. Over the past decades, domestic scholars represented by scholars such as *Wen Qiufang, Li Yuming, Zhang Tianwei, Shen Qi* and *Dai Manchun* have been making continuous efforts to explore the connotations and denotations of national language capacity based on China's national conditions, bringing up insightful views and made ground-breaking achievements.

© The Author(s), under exclusive license to Springer Nature Singapore Pte Ltd. 2024
X. Dong and J. Guo, *Chinese Rule of Law Path and Cultivation of Foreign-Related Rule of Law Talents*, https://doi.org/10.1007/978-981-97-2313-3_8

In the world where great changes have not been seen in a century, the reform of the global governance system is accelerating, and the international order is changing. China is brought into the limelight in the global stage. The new changes in the situation at home and abroad and the development of economy and society set higher requirements for the construction of foreign-related rule of law, which calls for the cultivation of foreign-related rule of law talents. On February 25, 2019, President Xi (2019) delivered a speech at the second plenary session of the Central Committee of the comprehensive rule of law, pointing out the necessity to speed up the construction of the legal system for the extraterritorial application of domestic laws, strengthen the cultivation of professional foreign-related rule of law talents, actively develop foreign-related legal services, strengthen corporate compliance awareness, and safeguard as well as serve a high level of opening up.

Improving national language capacity is an important goal of language planning in all countries in the world. The essence of this goal is an important human resource planning, so as to improve national language capacity (Shen and Zhao 2020: 47). It can be seen that the improvement of national language capacity and the cultivation of foreign-related rule of law talents complement and promote each other. Based on the theoretical framework of national language capacity, this paper points out the main problems and challenges in the cultivation of foreign-related rule of law talents in China and puts forward some suggestions to improve the cultivation of foreign-related rule of law talents in China, aiming to promote the mutual development of the cultivation of foreign-related rule of law talents and the construction of national language capacity.

8.2 Construction of National Language Capacity

1. Theoretical Framework of National Language Capacity

The concept of national language capacity was first put forward by *Brecht and Walton* in 1993. Richard and Ronald (1993) defined the concept of national language capacity as "the ability of a country to respond to specific language needs". In 2012, in the *Cambridge Handbook of Language Policy* compiled by Spolsky (2012: 10), a chapter discusses US language policy in defense and attack from the perspective of national language capacity. The study of national language capacity in the United States generally refers to the study of national foreign language (other than English) capacity. The National Foreign Language Center of the University of Maryland is such a research institution.

With the development of national construction and the proposal of various major strategies, the concept of "national language capacity" has entered the core of people's attention in China. *Li Yuming, Zhao Shiju, Wen Qiufang, Wei Hui, Yang Yiming, Su Jinzhi* and *Shen Qi* all discussed the basic issues such as the concept, nature and constituent elements of national language capacity, and constructed the conceptual system of national language capacity from the perspectives of sociolinguistics, language life, language management, language psychology and language education. Learning from scholars at home and abroad, Wen and Zhang (2018: 32) define national language capacity as "the language ability required by the government to deal with affairs involving national strategic interests at home and abroad."

In the first stage of the research of national language capacity, Wen and Zhang (2018: 33) divides the national language capacity into five dimensions as the evaluation indicators: management competence, which refers to the national competence to manage language affairs involving national strategic interests; monitoring competence, which refers to the national competence to control the language talent resources; innovational competence, which refers to the national competence to create language talent resources; productive competence, which refers to the national competence to develop language technology; expanding competence, which refers to the national competence to expand the international influence of the common language. In the second stage of national language capacity, *Wen Qiufang* redivides national language capacity into three dimensions: national language governance competence, national language core competence, and national language strategic competence.

2. Theoretical Framework of National Foreign-related Rule of law Language Capacity

The national foreign-related rule of law language capacity can be understood as the ability of the government to use legal language to deal with all affairs related to the national foreign-related rule of law. The national foreign-related rule of law language capacity is featured by internality and servability. Firstly, the foreign-related rule of law language capacity in the category of national language capacity is the internal language capacity of the country under idealized conditions, which is different from the discourse power already obtained in foreign-related rule of law affairs. Secondly, the characteristics of "servability" means the ability to meet the needs. To develop national foreign-related rule of law language capacity is to ensure the smooth implementation of foreign-related rule of law activities, better serving the construction of the rule of law in China. Specifically, it can be subdivided into five dimensions, and evaluation indicators and the explanations are shown in the Table 8.1.

3. National Language Capacity and National Foreign-related Rule of Law language Capacity

The relationship between national language capacity and national foreign-related rule of law language capacity is featured by inclusion, penetration, and coordination.

The first one is inclusion. National foreign-related rule of law language capacity is included in national language capacity. From the scope of the fields covered, the national foreign-related rule of law language capacity is an indispensable part of the national language capacity. National language capacity, which belongs to the branch of language sociology, includes national diplomatic language capacity, national military language capacity, national business language capacity, national

Table 8.1 Framework of national foreign-related rule of law language capacity

Sub-capacity	Evaluation indicator	Explanation
Governance competence	Power of organization	The government can establish a foreign-related rule of law language governance organization running from the central to the local level
	Power of coordination	There is an effective horizontal and vertical division of labor and cooperation between the foreign-related rule of law language governance system established by the government
	Power of execution	The foreign-related rule of law language governance organization system established by the government can implement the plans, give full play to their respective functions, and achieve desirable results
Monitoring competence	Power of coverage	The government, industries and universities can reserve foreign-related rule of law talents covering various languages and professional fields based on social needs
	Power of mastery	The government, industries and universities can establish a foreign-related rule of law talent pool and fully master the foreign-related rule of law talent resources
	Power of allocation	The government, industries and universities can accurately allocate foreign-related rule of law talent resources based on social needs
Standardization competence	Power of theory	The government, industries and universities can establish a systematic theory of foreign-related rule of law language standards
	Power of specification	The government, industries and universities can specify operable foreign-related rule of law language norms and standards
	Power of translation	The government, industries and universities can strengthen the management of legal translation projects to promote various exchanges and interactions
Education competence	Power of discipline	The government, industries and universities can follow up the construction of legal English discipline system at the macro level
	Power of science	The government, industries and universities can ensure the education system of foreign-related rule of law talents meets the internal regularity and social needs
	Power of teaching	The government, industries and universities can build a team of teachers with excellent comprehensive qualities, and strengthen the management of teaching materials, the compilation and updating of teaching materials

(continued)

Table 8.1 (continued)

Sub-capacity	Evaluation indicator	Explanation
Intelligence competence	Power of think tanks	The government, industries and universities can build think tanks for the construction of foreign-related rule of law language capacity and the cultivation of foreign-related rule of law talents
	Power of corpus	The government, industries and universities can build professional and intelligent laws and regulations retrieval corpus
	Power of platform	The government, industries and universities can build a learning platform to provide rich learning resources

news language capacity, national cultural language capacity, national rule of law language capacity, and so on.

The second one is penetration. With the deepening of reform and opening up and the implementation of China's "Going Global" strategy, the national foreign-related rule of law language capacity has penetrated into into the fields of diplomacy, business, culture, military and so on. The foreign-related rule of law language involves a wide range and its penetration is increasing. The construction of national foreign-related rule of law language capacity, which involves multidisciplinary backgrounds, is not only an important fulcrum of the development of national language capacity in other fields, which is conducive to realizing the complementary advantages of national language development in different fields, but also a key link to promote the development of national language capacity, which is beneficial for the national language capacity to develop towards a scientific, balanced and diversified direction.

The third one is coordination. The development of national language capacity requires multi-subject cooperation and multi-field coordination to provide language services, solve public problems and improve national capacity, which must involve the cooperation and coordination of different subject values and discourse forces in different fields. From a more in-depth perspective, the development of national language capacity and construction of the national foreign-related rule of law language capacity have formed a situation of mutual engagement, interdependence, shared difficulties and achievements, taking the improvement of the country's comprehensive power as the common goal.

4. Developing Foreign-related Rule of Law Language Capacity and Cultivating Foreign-related Rule of Law Talents

The sub-item capacity included in the development of national language capacity is not only an important part of national soft power, but also increasingly becomes a hard power to boost economic development, safeguard national interests and participate in global governance. Hard power and soft power are inseparable from the power of talents. If the foreign-related rule of law language capacity is an important power to tell Chinese Stories brilliantly and make the Chinese voice louder, then the foreign-related rule of law talents is undoubtedly the source of power.

For one thing, the language of the rule of law is the expression carrier of the construction of the rule of law. The national foreign-related rule of law language governance competence is an important national resource, the transformation of which can provide institutional guarantee and policy supply and implementation for the cultivation of foreign-related rule of law talents; monitoring competence can realize the forward-looking comprehensive coordination of talents and resources; standardization capacity can improve the language specification awareness of teachers, thus laying a foundation for the cultivation of foreign-related rule of law talents; education competence can ensure the scientificity of the cultivation mechanism of foreign-related rule of law talents; intelligence competence can promote the intellectualization of the cultivation of foreign-related rule of law talents.

For another, the cultivation of foreign-related rule of law talents will in turn promote the construction of national foreign-related rule of law language capacity. The development of national language capacity cannot be achieved overnight, but a process of dynamic management and coordinated development. During this process, outstanding foreign-related rule of law talents can provide powerful support for the development of national foreign-related rule of law language capacity, thus promoting the construction of national language capacity, serve the national development strategy and promote the construction of a global community of shared future.

5. Research Framework

Language planning is a great cause of each country. Dong (2020: 5) first proposes a framework of language planning based on "the Belt and Road" Initiative. On the basis of the framework of *Wen Qiufang*'s national language capacity and *Dong Xiaobo*'s language planning on "the Belt and Road" Initiative, the paper puts forward the framework of the cultivation of foreign-related rule of law talents from the perspective of national language capacity, as shown in Fig. 8.1. The state, industries, and academies, as the main subjective levels, are jointly committed to improving the national language foreign-related rule of law language capacity, so as to release joint efforts and stimulate vitality for the cultivation of foreign-related rule of law talents.

8.3 Cultivation of Foreign-Related Rule of Law Talents: Significance, Status Quo, and Problems to be Solved

1. Significance of Cultivating Foreign-Related Rule of Law Talents

The importance of foreign-related rule of law talents is mainly reflected in the following aspects:

The first one is to promote the construction of new liberal arts. In May 2018, *Wu Yan,* the director of the Department of higher education of the Ministry of education,

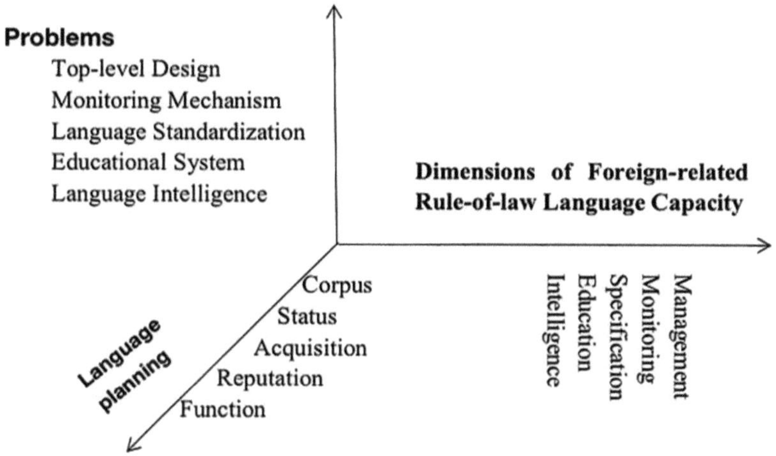

Fig. 8.1 Research framework of the cultivation of foreign-related rule of law talents from the perspective of national language capacity

formally put forward the concept of "new liberal arts". In May 2019, the Ministry of Education, the Committee of Political and Legislative Affairs, the Ministry of Science and Technology, and other departments jointly launched the "Six Excellence and One Top" Plan 2.0. "Six Excellence" includes "Excellent Rule of Law Talents". The construction of new liberal arts and the cultivation of foreign-related rule of law talents complement each other. The second one is to serve the national strategy. As "the Belt and Road" Initiative has been promoted, the importance of legal services has become increasingly prominent. Chinese foreign-related rule of law talents can more accurately understand customers' demands and provide high-quality and efficient services. The third one is to safeguard national interests. Since 2018, trade frictions between China and the United States have been escalating, and many Chinese enterprises are facing new uncertainties. The cultivation of foreign-related rule of law talents is not only to help Chinese enterprises master international commercial arbitration rules, mediate or arbitrate international commercial disputes, cultivate enterprise compliance culture and prevent the "Going Global" risk of Chinese enterprises, but also to deal with international trade protectionism and safeguard national development interests. The fourth one is to participate in global governance. The rule of law is the basic way of governing the country, the basic guarantee of economic construction, an important part of core national strength and the ultimate strategic goal of national development (Wang 2016: 16). Foreign related rule of law talents are an important supporting force for China to actively participate in global governance, become defenders and builders of international rules, enhance its voice in international affairs and promote the construction of a global community of shared future.

2. Status Quo of the Cultivation of Foreign-related Rule of Law Talents

In recent years, the Chinese government has issued a series of policies related to foreign-related laws and the cultivation of foreign-related rule of law talents. President *Xi Jinping* proposed for the first time in the second meeting of the Central Committee of the comprehensive rule of law in February 25, 2019 that "professionals in the field of rule of law" should be cultivated. Since the 18th Party Congress, *Xi Jinping* has made several important speeches on the construction of the rule of law and the cultivation of rule of law talents, pointing out that to participate in international affairs as a responsible big country, while heading for the world, China must be good at applying the rule of law, which calls for the cultivation of foreign-related rule of law professionals (Zheng and Jiang 2021: 4). It can be seen that the cultivation of foreign legal talents has become and will always be an urgent work and a national strategy for a long time in the future.

At the university level, the General Office of the Ministry of Education and the Committee of Political and Legislative Affairs and the Ministry of Education (2012) issued the notice on "*the First List of Outstanding Legal Talents Education and Cultivation Bases*" in 2012, approving 22 universities such as China University of Political Science and Law as foreign-related legal talents education and cultivation bases. In 2021, China University of Political Science and Law began to carry out the program with Beijing Foreign Studies University. The students majoring in foreign-related rule of law in the School of International Law study in Beijing Foreign Studies University in the second academic year. Those who meet the degree awarding standards of the two universities will be awarded a Joint Bachelor's Degree.

3. Problems to Be Solved in the Cultivation of Foreign-related Rule of Law Talents

The fist problem is the lack of top-level design. The Top-level design is a design method of systematic promotion from top to bottom. Specifically, top-level design is to systematically configure and combine various elements and formulate implementation paths and strategies from a global perspective (Ji 2001: 40). The lack of top-level design in the cultivation of foreign-related rule of law talents is reflected in the fact that there is a great shortage of talents with high-level English or less commonly taught language skills and rule of law professional knowledge. With the development of the times and the progress of society, economic activities are in line with international standards, but legal work can not keep up with the pace of the development of the times (Li 2014: 90). By the end of 2020, there were more than 522, 000 lawyers in China. However, according to the national roster of 1000 foreign-related lawyers compiled by the Ministry of Justice (2018), only 985 outstanding foreign-related lawyers are included (Wen and Zhang 2018: 36).

The second problem is the lack of monitoring mechanism. There are two indicators to measure monitoring control competence: mastery and allocation. Mastery is the basis and premise of allocation, which refers to the comprehensive mastery of national language talent resources by relevant national management institutions. Allocation refers to "the speed and accuracy of invoking language resources to serve national needs".

The imbalance of monitoring mechanism is reflected in the imperfect evaluation mechanism of foreign-related rule of law language ability. At present, CET-4, CET-6,

TEM-4, CET-8, IELTS and TOEFL are mainly used to test students' general English level. They are not competent for the evaluation of professional legal English level. The National Unified Examination of Legal English Certificate (LEC), organized and implemented by China University of Political Science and Law and Beijing Foreign Studies University, is the only examination to investigate foreign-related rule of law talents, but it has not been widely promoted and implemented as a vocational admission examination. The language evaluation standards for foreign-related rule of law talents in other languages except English are still in the blank stage.

In order to enhance the allocation of talents, the government and other departments has carried out the construction of foreign-related rule of law talent pools, but there are also some problems in the current talent pools. Four search items are set up in the national 1000 foreign lawyer talent query system, which are province, working language, business field and keyword query. The collection of practical experience, business skills, research direction, interest direction, honor and other information of talents is not detailed enough. There is only a general business direction for query. When talents are really needed, it is difficult to accurately match demands with talent skills. At the same time, dynamic management is not implemented to activate talent pool. After the establishment of some talent pools, it is still a static information structure. There is no regular inventory, summary and analysis to judge the demand and supply of foreign legal talents. It has not become a dynamic talent information structure through internal communication and sharing.

The third problem is nonstandard use of legal Language. Firstly, the legislative language of China's foreign-related laws and regulations is lack of standardization. In 2009, the legal working committee of the Standing Committee of the National People's Congress promulgated the legislative technical specifications I. In 2011, the legislative technical specifications II further standardized some commonly used legal terms that are mixed or inconsistent in legislative practice. However, ten years have passed since the promulgation of the legislative technical specifications in 2011. Some legal provisions have not been revised in time according to the specifications. Secondly, the judicial language of foreign-related laws and regulations is lack of standardization. Judicial language standardization means that the language used by national judicial organs and their judicial personnel to deal with cases in accordance with legal functions and powers and legal procedures must be standardized, which is of exemplary significance for the cultivation of foreign-related rule of law talents. There are many deficiencies in the content and form of China's foreign-related civil and commercial adjudication documents, such as non-uniform format and non-standard language (Song and Zhao 2011: 115). There are also problems existing in the production of foreign-related maritime judgment documents, among which the problems related to language standardization are that the accuracy of expression is not enough (Dang 2019: 62). So far, the standards on judicial language have not been systematically formulated and widely implemented. Thirdly, there is a lack of theoretical and practical research on the standardization of foreign-related rule of law language translation. Any research to be carried out in depth must be based on strong theories. However, at present, there is almost no unified legal language translation standards. At the same time, there is a relative lack of criticism on legal translation. There are only a small number of works and articles focusing on criticism of legal translation. Legal translation lacks the environment of collective criticism and research, making its development slow, even errors and problems emerge one after another, which hinders the teaching and learning of foreign-related rule of law.

The fourth problem is that the education system is not perfect. Firstly, the current cultivating objectives are broad and lack of characteristics. At present, the training objectives of foreign-related rule of law talents in colleges and universities are highly homogeneous, such as "high quality", "innovative talents" and "compound talents". Few colleges and universities position the objectives as cultivating foreign-related rule of law talents who meet the needs of the local region or specific industries. At the same time, the connection between cultivating objectives and national strategies still needs to be strengthened. There are many talents familiar with the legal system of developed countries such as Europe and America, but few talents equipped themselves with knowledge of laws along the "the Belt and Road".

Secondly, there is a lack of diversified cooperation in modes of education. For one thing, the cooperation is limited to some western countries or some developed areas, while there are few cooperation projects with the countries along "the Belt and Road". For another, universities do not pay enough attention to resource integration, lack of awareness and continued action of resource integration among schools, universities, and interaction and communication with practical departments.

Thirdly, the curriculum system design cannot meet the requirements of the knowledge structure of foreign-related rule of law talents. According to the training objectives, the law schools of some colleges and universities mostly focus on international law, while there are few foreign-related rule of law courses on laws of countries along "the Belt and Road" and the political, economic, cultural and religious aspects of these countries. In addition, the design of curriculum system lacks practicality. Some colleges and universities in China do not pay enough attention to the foreign-related rule of law practice courses, the arrangement of foreign-related rule of law practice simulation is insufficient, and the cases involved in the course are mainly developed countries such as Europe and the United States, and less classic cases of countries along "the Belt and Road".

Fourthly, the compilation and publishing of teaching materials cannot keep up with the pace of the development of the times. Initially, there is a lack of clear guiding ideology: some focus on legal knowledge or English skills, while others on other professional knowledge based on legal English. Besides, there is a lack of foreign case teaching materials. The majority of cases are selected from foreign countries, and there are few cases of foreign-related classical cases in China, which negatively affects the cultivation of students' ability to correctly analyze the legal problems arising from China's foreign exchanges through foreign-related case teaching. Furthermore, timeliness and practicability are not high. Some newly published textbooks or reference books do not incorporate the latest American precedents and some influential case materials, which is not conducive for learners to grasp the latest judicial trends in Britain and the United States. Last but not least, there is a lack of audio-visual and other multimedia materials. Most legal English textbooks still focus on reading, writing and translation, with little or no involvement in listening and speaking.

Fifthly, there are many deficiencies in the construction of teaching staff for the cultivation of foreign-related rule of law talents. Among the teachers of the law school, apart from those who teach international law, other teachers mainly focus on domestic fields, and lack international vision and international communication ability. At the same time, most of the teachers in the school of foreign languages have accumulated rich experience in the teaching of general English, but very few teachers can teach legal foreign languages and are familiar with foreign-related legal culture.

The last problem is the lack of intelligence in language. In 2015, UNESCO adopted the 2030 action framework for education, which makes specific plans to achieve the goal of "inclusive and equitable quality education for all and lifelong learning" by 2030, requiring "the use of appropriate education and teaching methods and appropriate information technology". Colleges and universities also see the benefits of new technology to teaching and cultivation of talents. Mobile learning, as a new learning method, provides a platform support for the teaching of foreign language. However, many mobile learning platforms provide supports for the teaching and learning of English for general purposes rather than legal English. Due to the lack of real language application environment, legal English teaching has been limited to classroom teaching for a long time. It still takes time to realize the deep integration of information technology and legal foreign language teaching.

At the same time, although some domestic universities have built corpora related with legal English, the corpora they have built are either small in scale, limited in reference significance, or inconvenient to be made public due to copyright or other underlying reasons. The practical effect of the corpus built by a single institution or individual for the cultivation of foreign-related rule of law talents is very limited, not to mention extend the corpus to the national level.

The scientific research achievements of think tanks, such as monographs, papers, translations and consulting reports, are the raw materials for the cultivation of talents (Dong and Hu 2021: 26). However, some universities, industries, and practical departments have not made joint and continued efforts to build foreign-related rule of law construction think tanks to facilitate teaching with systematic professional knowledge and promote the cultivation of foreign-related rule of law talents.

8.4 Suggestions for Cultivation of Foreign-Related Rule of Law Talents

1. Developing Governance Competence

Language status planning is a social planning, which is generally defined as a planning that pays attention to the relationship between language and other aspects of social life. Zhou (2005: 53) pointed out that the status planning will affect the role of a language in society, configure some new functions for the language, and make it become the language of teaching media or official language through the implementation of the planning. The premise of status planning of foreign-related rule of law language is a perfect organization to manage foreign-related rule of law language.

The first is to strengthen the power of organization. At present, the construction and development of China's national language capacity still lacks a strong administrative governance system. It is suggested to expand the functions of the existing National Language Commission, uniformly managing domestic and foreign language related affairs, implement the task of improving national language capacity, and work according to the new external situation. In view of the strong professionalism of the development of foreign-related language capacity and the cultivation of foreign-related rule of law talents, it is suggested that a "Project-based Team for Cultivating Foreign-related Rule of Law Talents" be established under the Central Committee for the comprehensive rule of law, with the Committee of Political and Legislative Affairs, the Central Office for the Rule of Law, the Supreme People's Court, the Central Organization Department of the Supreme People's Procuratorate, the Ministry of Education, the Ministry of Justice, and the Ministry of Public Security as the leading units.

The second is to strengthen the power of coordination. The "Project-based Team for Cultivating Foreign-related Rule of Law Talents" is responsible for coordinating internal resources, internal institutional relations, and various branches and personnel within the organization. There are different divisions of labor within its organizational system. The smooth performance of its functions, the cultivation of foreign-related rule of law talents, and the promotion of the construction of national foreign-related rule of law language capacity are inseparable from the rationality of internal division of labor and the coordination of internal organizations.

Horizontal coordination, which refers to the division and coordination of different functional departments, should be ensured to strengthen the overall coordination, giving full play to the role of government departments, universities, courts, procuratorates, law firms and enterprises in the cultivation of foreign-related rule of law talents, so as to realize the coverage and orientation of macro language governance. The Ministry of Justice and Ministry of Education should further strengthen communication and coordination, fully summarize the successful experience of cross management of legal education, carefully design the internal organizational structure, pay attention to integrity and professionalism, and establish an operation mode of mutual coordination and appropriate separation of decision-making, implementation and supervision.

Vertical coordination, ranging from the decisions-making to the implementation, should also be coordinated. From the perspective of language governance level, provinces, autonomous regions, municipalities directly under the central government and special administrative regions should first firmly establish the awareness of the overall situation and the concept of the overall situation, so as to ensure the specific implementation of the central foreign-related rule of law language policy and foreign-related rule of law talent cultivating policy, as well as explore and innovate according to national policies and local realities, striving to cultivate the talents with local characteristics.

The third is to strengthen the power of execution. The ultimate goal of planning is to serve practice. A high-level implementation of execution is key to the cultivation of foreign-related rule of law talents. Without strong executive power, no matter how perfect and scientific the decision-making scheme might be, it could not be transformed into reality. In addition to establishing the specific status of foreign-related rule of law language with the help of normative documents issued by national decision-making organs, the Ministry of Education and Committee of Political and Legislative Affairs need to coordinate and solve the problems in the implementation of the foreign-related rule of law talent training plan. When formulating policies related to talent training, local education departments and political and legal departments should, based on the current situation, design a highly operable executive system for the cultivation of foreign-related rule of law talents, promote the dismantling action of universities, ensure continuous feedback and effective implementation. Local education departments and political and legal departments should strengthen the tracking management of the implementation process of the cultivating plan for foreign-related rule of law talents, strengthen dynamic monitoring, grasp the work progress, take the three links of operation, monitoring and correction as the core, pay attention to seriousness and flexibility, analyze problems with a scientific attitude so as to create a desirable operation atmosphere for the implementation and operation of executive power.

2. Developing Monitoring Competence

The national foreign-related rule of law language monitoring competence refers to the country's familiarity with foreign-related rule of law talent resources and ability to effectively make full use of foreign-related rule of law talent resources. The establishment of foreign-related rule of law talent pool is one of the effective ways to improve the national foreign-related rule of law language monitoring competence, whose sub capacity shall be composed of coverage, mastery and allocation.

The first is to strengthen the power of coverage. All types of talents should be covered. The foreign-related rule of law team is composed of "specialized team for foreign-related rule of law", "foreign-related rule of law service team" and "teaching and researching team for foreign-related rule of law". The "specialized team for foreign-related rule of law" mainly includes legislators, judges and prosecutors of the International Court of Justice who participate in global governance and international legislation; The "foreign-related rule of law service team" mainly includes foreign lawyers, foreign notaries and foreign mediators; The "teaching and researching team for foreign-related rule of law" mainly includes educators and researchers engaged in international law and the extraterritorial application of Chinese law in universities and scientific research institutions.

A national foreign-related rule of law talent pool covering key languages talent types should be established. Key languages are a relatively open dynamic system for a certain period of time, which can help countries continuously adjust the status and internal relationship of various languages in the education system based on the specific needs of different periods. The main language of the foreign-related rule of law is the Chinese, English, French, Russian, Arabic and Spanish, and the specially needed language closely related to national interests, such as the language of the neighboring countries and the languages of countries along "the Belt and Road", languages of major trading partners and languages of hostile countries.

A national foreign-related rule of law talent pool covering the types of talents in core fields should be established. Language function planning is to plan the value and function of language phenomena at each functional level, and its task is to plan the language function at each functional level. Language functions are divided into eight levels: national language, official working language, education, mass media, public service, public communication, culture and daily communication (Li 2008). In terms of planning for the coverage of the rule of law in the field of foreign affairs, China should have its own strategy of "key areas" covering foreign affairs, including the business areas that have been laid out.

The second is to strengthen the power of mastery. The use of foreign-related rule of law talents is based on the power of mastery. On the basis of knowing the number of languages of foreign-related rule of law talents in China, how many languages in the world they can communicate directly, and how many fields they can play their functions, the state includes the above talents into the foreign-related rule of law talent pool for management, establishes detailed personal information files for them, and adds single search to facilitate dispatch and use by different functional departments at any time, to improve the accuracy of talent transfer and to make use of the gathering and radiation effect of talents. Using scientific and technological means such as artificial intelligence, Internet and big data analysis to realize the in-depth excavation of the demand for foreign-related rule of law services and the scientific matching of the recommendation of foreign-related rule of law talents, so as to effectively integrate and access high-quality foreign-related rule of law service resources throughout the country and even the world.

The third is to strengthen the power of allocation. It is necessary to enhance the formation of foreign-related rule of law talent team. The foreign legal industry tends to be team-oriented, and coordinated development tends to be a wise move. The effectiveness of the overall foreign-related rule of law talent team is not necessarily equal to the sum of everyone's effectiveness, which can be greater than or less than the sum of everyone's effectiveness. The difference depends on whether the system combination is reasonable. A mature and efficient foreign-related rule of law service team, like other efficient teams, will have clear role sharing in different stages. In different stages of foreign-related rule of law service, the core is division of labor, cooperation and connection. In specific business, different foreign-related rule of law service teams needs to be established, such as a "short and fast" team, a team good at process division and handling many litigation procedures, as well as a perennial foreign-related rule of law adviser team.

3. Developing Standardization Competence

The corpus planning of the national foreign-related rule of law language refers to the formulation of foreign-related rule of law language norms and translation standards.

Law regulates people's behavior, but it must first be regulated by language. Language standardization is the premise of effectively regulating human behavior (Liao 2008). The following aspects are the focus of corpus planning.

The first is to strengthen the power of theory. The standardization of foreign-related rule of law language is of great significance to the construction of foreign-related rule of law language system in China. Without theory, there would be no in-depth research. As for the standardization of foreign-related rule of law language, the cross application of theory should be strengthened. The construction of standardized theory of foreign-related rule of law language is based on the active study and exploration of foreign-related rule of law language theories, starting with corpus planning in the legal field, breaking the single research situation of law, sociology, politics and linguistics, carrying out legal linguistics research combined with the actual situation of the field, implementing the planning and translation norms of legal terms, finding a suitable theory that can be used for reference and apply it to the study of legal language, and then to the study of foreign-related rule of law language. The development of foreign-related rule of law language needs the organic integration of law and foreign language, so the potential barriers between law and languages are needed to be broken in order to absorb the theoretical literacy of the two disciplines to enrich the research perspective theory. What is more, learning from the western legal and language research theories is also an advisable way.

The second is to strengthen the power of specification. Legal language, as the carrier of legal culture, also carries the publicity and education role of legal culture. Promoting the correct expression of legal language and making people better understand the role of law on protection of the rights and obligations of the public, which is conducive to the publicity and education of law. Due to the stability, universality and far-reaching influence of Chinese, legal language should become a model of modern Chinese. It is a serious task for every legal worker to temper legal language and use standardized modern Chinese. In order to deeply and comprehensively participate in international affairs, international authoritative experts should be called to establish an association for the rule of law language norms to promote the theoretical improvement of legal language norms, making good use of administrative resources, establishing a collection and response mechanism for standardized application problems, and regularly collecting the language standardization problems and opinions of front-line users in various application fields, so as to understand the main puzzles and ideas and avoid excessive accumulation of negative opinions.

The third is to strengthen the power of translation. In terms of the standardization of foreign-related rule of law language translation, members from Translators of China should study the standards and norms of legal translation, the teaching of legal translation, the ability requirements and evaluation methods of legal language translators and interpreters. At the same time, an internal academic criticism system of legal translation should be established. Academic criticism can supervise and promote the healthy development of academic research. Academic translation also needs corresponding translation criticism. However, in the past decades, translated works have come into being one after another, but there is a relative lack of criticism and discussion on legal translation. There are only a few works and articles devoted to legal translation and criticism of translated works. Legal translation lacks the environment of collective appreciation and criticism. Therefore, it is urgent to establish reasonable procedural rules and substantive standards of legal translation criticism system.

4. Developing Education Competence

Acquisition planning, also known as language education planning, refers to the learning objectives that users must achieve, which are generally completed through a systematic teaching system. The essence of acquisition planning is the measures taken to cultivate and maintain the language proficiency of individuals and even groups. Acquisition planning includes the formulation of macro policies and specific programs, as well as the preparation of teaching materials to promote the development of individual and group language skills, so as to meet the future uses of the language and its social, institutional and individual needs (Dong 2020).

The first is to strengthen the power of discipline. Legal English, based on general English, is a language with professional characteristics formed and used in legislation, judicature and other law-related activities to express legal scientific concepts and engage in litigation or non-litigation legal affairs (Zhang 2019). According to the Catalog of Undergraduate Majors in Colleges and Universities, Legal English should belong to "foreign language and literature" (first-class discipline) in "Literature" (discipline category). The secondary disciplines under the first discipline include dozens of foreign languages such as English, Russian and French, as well as translation and business English, but there is no secondary discipline of "legal English". It is worth noting that legal English, which is very similar to business English, should have an independent secondary discipline direction. Weng and Weng (2012) pointed out that the reason why business English can become an independent discipline direction is that business English is a new discipline differentiated from English, which is obviously distinct from general English. According to the laws of discipline development, it is natural for business English to be separated from English. Obviously, according to the characteristics of legal English, we should position it as a subject direction parallel to business English (Zhang 2019).

Many colleges and universities in China have set up the major direction of legal English. At this stage, it is necessary to analyze the current situation, sort out the existing problems, advantages and disadvantages of the new major, and put forward clear, phased and practical goals and measures in combination with the actual situation of the school and the new major. The general idea, guiding ideology and basic principles of new major construction should be reflected in the construction plan of the new major, the construction objectives and cycle should be clear.

The second is to strengthen the power of science. Science power refers to whether the training of language talents conforms to the law of discipline (Wen and Zhang 2018). The revision of the training program for foreign-related rule of law talents needs to be promoted at the school level, major level and curriculum level. The focus of the school level is to determine the training concept, training orientation and training framework, and the core is the training concept; The focus of the major level is to determine the training mode, training scheme and platform construction, and the core is the training scheme; The focus of the curriculum level is to determine the teaching mode and textbook construction, and the core is the teaching mode.

The first premise of ensuring the science power of major construction is to ensure that language talents comply with the discipline regularity. The construction of Legal English major is based on introducing professional decision-making mechanism, taking various forms such as hearings, seminars and demonstration meetings, and comprehensively considering the following factors: first, the social demand for foreign-related rule of law talents, including the talent market demand of the whole country and even the whole international community in the next 5–10 years. The second is the school running conditions, including the existing teachers who can teach legal English, the existing internship conditions, and the school's human, material and financial resources. The third is the effectiveness and efficiency of establishing the discipline: how to give full play to the potential of the existing disciplines and teaching resources of the school to improve the construction of the discipline and the overall running level of the school.

The second is to ensure the science power of curriculum. The professional curriculum system of Legal English includes "general courses, English language knowledge courses, legal English knowledge courses, and legal English skills and Practice Courses". In the curriculum design of legal English, the total class hours of four-year professional courses shall not be less than 1900 class hours (excluding public compulsory courses and elective courses), and students' tasks related with extracurricular reading, self-study, innovation programs, internship and independent development (as appropriate according to specific courses) shall be stipulated (Zhang 2019). With regard to the issue of Legal English teaching time, in addition to the guarantee of explicit time or teaching hours, the effective use of classroom unit time and the use of extracurricular learning time should also be considered.

Thirdly, school orientation needs to ensure science power. The talent training objectives of colleges and universities at different levels have certain similarities and differences. They should develop their strengths and avoid weaknesses, dislocation competition, and multiple disorder in school development, talent training due to excessive homogenization. For instance, colleges and universities at the first level have excellent comprehensive strength, and should focus on cultivating elite foreign-related rule of law talents with the ability to lead social development, such as rule of law diplomatic talents or famous international lawyers; colleges and universities at the second level have relatively strong comprehensive strength and obvious characteristic advantages, and should focus on cultivating talents with certain characteristics who serve a certain region or field.

The third is to strengthen the power of teaching. The power of teaching is mainly reflected in the improvement of teaching materials and teachers. Teaching materials are the carrier of knowledge, and teachers are the premise of major establishment. High quality teaching materials that meet the needs of foreign-related rule of law talent training should not only highlight foreign-related features, but also reflect China's local features such as economy, law and culture, and meet China's national conditions. Therefore, the compilation of foreign-related rule of law language teaching materials must start with the characteristics and teaching regularities and focus on the needs of learners.

First, the synchronization of bilingual textbooks for beginners. It is suggested that the compilation of English-Chinese bilingual textbooks should adopt the English-Chinese comparison mode of half-Chinese and half-English in terms of language matching. From the current teaching practice, bilingual teaching materials in international law courses, can not only help learners in the first stage understand the rules of international law deeply because they are familiar with their mother tongue, but also master the English expression of the corresponding expression in English. Secondly, the synchronization of foreign-related case teaching materials. Another feature of the training curriculum of foreign-related rule of law talents is to be practical. Case study is one of the main forms of foreign-related rule of law practice curriculum. The case teaching material suitable for the foreign-related case teaching mode is a comprehensive carrier combining the course contents and teaching methods. During the construction of "the Belt and Road", there are many lessons that can be learned, so if case textbooks include some typical cases related with foreign-related affairs, students will undoubtedly benefit from them, deepening understanding of the knowledge and improving abilities to solve practical problems.

Teachers also constitute an important part of the power of teaching. It is the top priority for the cultivation of foreign-related rule of law talents to establish a professional teacher echelon with a reasonable structure, which calls for the adherence to the principle of "teacher-oriented", constant improvement of the discipline and professional leadership system, strengthening of the construction of backbone teachers, and training of young and middle-aged teachers in a planned and purposeful way. There are two links that to be grasped: attraction and training. In terms of attraction, colleges and universities should strengthen the introduction, formulate various preferential conditions, attract high-level teachers to work in the school, supplement the shortage of professional teachers, especially actively introduce discipline professional leaders and backbone curriculum teachers urgently needed for the cultivation of foreign-related rule of law talents, further optimize the team structure of core teachers of new majors, make full use of the existing teacher resources and social resources in the school, and hire experts in enterprises, scientific research institutes, government management departments and other professionals with rich practical experience and considerable theoretical level as distinguished professors, part-time professors, visiting professors and part-time teachers of the new specialty, which can not only solve the contradiction of the shortage of professional teachers, but also make up for the defect of weak practical links. Regarding training, the structure of teachers can be optimized and the overall level and quality of teachers can be improved through on-the-job short-term training, further study, self-study, visiting schools, pursuing degrees, academic exchanges and other forms.

5. Strengthen Intelligence Competence

In 1983, *Howard Gardmer*, an American developmental psychologist, put forward the theory of "Multiple Intelligences", one of which is language intelligence which is closely associated with memorizing information in oral and written language, reading and writing, debate and persuasion, and explaining things clearly. "Internet+Education" accelerated the pace of educational informationization and intelligence and changed the traditional way of learning and training in colleges and universities. In terms of the intelligence construction of foreign-related rule of law language, the construction of think tanks, corpora and learning platforms should be the focus.

The first is to strengthen the power of think tanks. Think tanks refer to "research and analysis of public policies, participation in formulation process, and policy recommendations on domestic and international affairs related to policies." The "think tank" is an organization that provides advice to decision-makers and urges them to make correct decisions (Zhu and Jiang 2016). Think tanks established by universities and industries are the support of the training structure system of foreign-related rule of law talents. Learners constantly improve their professional skills and expand their knowledge on this platform. At the same time, Think Tanks also play the function of solving problems and making suggestions for decision-making departments and can put forward targeted suggestions on new problems in the training of foreign-related rule of law talents. Building corresponding think tanks is indispensable for the cultivation of foreign-related rule of law talents. For the cultivation of foreign-related rule of law talents, the cooperation and exchange of relevant think tanks will be an effective means to integrate the advantages of think tanks, share think tank resources and highlight the characteristics of think tanks (Liu and Zhou 2020).

The second is to strengthen the power of corpus. Firstly, corpora on legal foreign language translation should be established. In view of the singleness and limitation of the types of translation examples in teaching materials, how to obtain rich and diverse appropriate translation examples is a major problem. The use of corpora can undoubtedly solve this problem. Using the massive monolingual corpus and bilingual parallel corpus on the Internet, learners can easily retrieve a large number of real and fresh translation examples. Through observation and group discussion, learners can summarize relevant language translation skills, explore translation laws, and effectively reverse the situation of passive learning in traditional translation teaching (Cai and Yu 2021: 88). In addition, It is advisable to establish foreign-related rule of law language learners corpora, collecting students' translation homework, foreign-related rule of law papers, classroom exercises, etc. to form corpus texts, make a quantitative analysis of students' language use, so as to grasp the teaching effects and improve the quality of teaching. Finally, a multi-modal corpus should be established. Multi-modal corpus refers to the corpus after manually labeling various modal forms such as sound, image, action, gesture and facial expression (Yang and Wu 2012: 72). Through the multimodal corpus, learners can easily extract the corpus on the same topic for horizontal comparison, such as the expression habits of lawyers in different countries on the theme of "enterprise compliance" in the same trial, or the vertical comparison of the interpretation languages of the same legal translator in previous courts and analyze their discourse style and fixed expression. In the horizontal and vertical comparison, students can fully learn and master the discourse knowledge of foreign legal language, such as structure, connection, development, language and so on.

The third is to strengthen the power of platform. In the era of digital information, the development and promotion of APP represents the rapid rise of new communication applications and has become an important development direction in the Internet era. The development of APP learning platform is concerned by more and more people. The current app development is mainly aimed at general foreign languages. If the foreign-related rule of law language learning platform can be built, learners will have easier access to a variety of language learning materials. Besides, as a new and powerful educational technology, VR has brought new opportunities for learners to improve learners' comprehensive application ability of English, which has been verified by many empirical studies (Li et al. 2019: 82). In the virtual environment, learners can naturally acquire foreign-related rule of law language through vivid interactive experience. For beginners, some courses with interactive interpretation or a small amount of English interpretation combined with court video can be introduced to fully mobilize learners' enthusiasm and initiative in legal foreign language. For learners with a certain foundation, a language teaching environment with a high sense of immersion and natural interaction can be provided to encourage learners to participate, such as voice input of English sentences, and the platform also provides feedback in the form of voice.

8.5 Conclusion

In May 2021, President Xi (2019) stressed in the thirtieth collective learning of the Political Bureau of the CPC Central Committee. "To tell the story of China well and to display a real, three-dimensional and comprehensive China is an important task to strengthen the construction of international communication capacity". According to Yao (2018), reputation planning refers to consciously creating a superior social psychological environment to improve the social reputation of language. It is an action strategy of status planning, which is usually realized through communication and promotion. At the same time, he believes that reputation planning monitors language planning behavior and focuses on the improvement of language positive attitude. Comprehensively improving the effectiveness of international communication and building a strong team of professionals to meet the needs of international communication in the new era are inseparable from foreign-related rule of law language planning. Building a foreign discourse system and promoting the expression of Chinese stories and Chinese voices are inseparable from foreign-related rule of law talents.

Language construction is the grand plan of our country, and talent training is the foundation of our country. Cultivating foreign-related rule of law talents and promoting the construction of national language capacity is not only the need to improve the country's comprehensive national strength, but also the need to help build a global community of shared future. The five kinds of competence under the national language capacity—governance, monitoring, standardization, education, and intelligence—have priority development considerations, but do not necessarily show a simple linear development relationship. Their corresponding training programs for foreign-related rule of law talents can develop cooperatively and promote each other.

The construction and development of national language capacity largely depends on the construction of talent training system. Foreign-related rule of law talents are not only legal talents, but also language talents, who are one of the important forces in the construction of national language capacity.

References

Cai, Y., and X. Yu. 2021. A study on corps-based translation teaching model in backdrop of "Internet +." *Journal of Yichun University* 5: 88–89.

Committee of Political and Legislative Affairs and the Ministry of Education. 2012. The first list of outstanding legal talents education and cultivation bases. Retrieved 1 Oct 2021, from http://www.gov.cn/zwgk/2012-12/19/content_2293555.htm

Dang, D. 2019. On the normative path of foreign-related maritime judgment documents. *Shantou University Journal (humanities and Social Sciences Edition)* 3: 62–68.

Dong, X. 2020. The contents and methods in Chinese language planning research based on "the belt and road" initiative. *Foreign Language Learning Theory and Practice* 1: 1–8.

Dong, X., and B. Hu. 2021. Problems of and solutions to the cultivation of foreign-related rule-of-law talents under the guidance of Xi Jinping's thought on rule of law. *Rule of Law in Jiangsu* 4: 26–31.

Ji, D. 2001. Top level design: a new perspective of talent training in colleges and universities. *China Higher Education* 7: 40–42.

Li, Y. 2008. A discussion on language function planning. *Applied Linguistics*, 1, 2–8. https://doi.org/10.16499/j.cnki.1003-5397.2008.01.001

Li, G. 2014. Studying the status quo and development of legal English in China with special reference to lawyer industry in Guangzhou. *Journal of Guangdong University of Foreign Studies* 4: 90–91.

Li, B., Wang, Y., and Ren, Y. 2019. Effects of virtual reality on students' academic achievements: meta-analysis of 40 experiments and quasi-experiments. *Open Education Research*, 4, 82–90. https://doi.org/10.13966/j.cnki.kfjyyj.2019.04.009

Liao, M. 2008. My views on problems of legal language standardization in China. *Rhetoric Learning*, 5, 30–36. https://doi.org/10.16027/j.cnki.cn31-2043/h.2008.05.017

Liu, C., and Zhou, J. 2020. Research on the cultivation of foreign-related rule-of-law talents under the characteristic national think tanks. *Journal of Bohai University (Philosophy and Social Sciences Edition)*, 6, 136–140. https://doi.org/10.13831/j.cnki.issn.1672-8254.2020.06.026

Ministry of Justice. 2018. National talent query system for thousands of foreign-related lawyers. Retrieved 12 Jun 2023, from http://www.bcisz.org/plug/lawyerquery/

Richard, D.B., and W. Ronald. 1993. National strategic planning in the less commonly taught languages. *The Annals of the American Academy of Political and Social Science* 17: 532–540.

Shen, Q., and D. Zhao. 2020. National language capacity planning in the perspective of global governance. *Journal of Yunnan Normal University (philosophy and Social Science Edition)* 3: 47–53.

Song, L., and Z. Zhao. 2011. On the existing problems of China's foreign-related civil and commercial adjudication documents. *China Law Review* 1: 115–120.

Spolsky, B. 2012. *The Cambridge handbook of language policy*. Cambridge University Press.

Wang, Z. 2016. *Law, rule of law and legal education.* Law Press.

Wen, Q., and Zhang, T. 2018. *Developing a theoretical framework of national language capacity.* Peking University Press.
Weng, J., and Weng, F. 2012. Business English studies: its concept as a discipline and its disciplinary attribute. *Foreign Languages in China*, 5, 4–6. https://doi.org/10.13564/j.cnki.issn.1672-9382.2012.05.011
Xi, J. (2019, February 26). *A speech made by President Xi Jinping at the Second Meeting of the Commission for Law-based Governance under the CPC Central Committee.* People's Daily.
Yang, L., and Z. Wu. 2012. Construction and implementation of multi-media news corpus based on web-design model for listening teaching and research. *Modern Information Technology* 8: 72–76.
Yao, Z. 2018. Reflections on China's current language situation and language planning. *Language Planning*, 12, 56–58. https://doi.org/10.16412/j.cnki.1001-8476.2018.12.019
Zhang, F. 2019. On the subject orientation of legal English. *Foreign Languages in China,* 2, 4–9. https://doi.org/10.13564/j.cnki.issn.1672-9382.2019.02.002
Zheng, Y., and Jiang, B. 2021. Four dimensions of strengthening the cultivation of foreign-related rule-of-law talents. *Guangming Daily.*
Zhou, Q. 2005. Theoretical schools and thoughts of foreign language planning. *Journal of World Peoples Studies* 4: 53–54.
Zhu, H., and Y. Jiang. 2016. Current status and future strategy of think tanks in Chinese colleges and universities. *Journal of Higher Education Management* 2: 47–54.

MIX
Papier aus verantwortungsvollen Quellen
Paper from responsible sources
FSC® C105338

If you have any concerns about our products,
you can contact us on
ProductSafety@springernature.com

In case Publisher is established outside the EU,
the EU authorized representative is:
Springer Nature Customer Service Center GmbH
Europaplatz 3, 69115 Heidelberg, Germany

Printed by Libri Plureos GmbH
in Hamburg, Germany